*Mastering the Chopin Etudes
and Other Essays*

ABBY WHITESIDE

Mastering the Chopin Etudes and Other Essays

Edited by Joseph Prostakoff and Sophia Rosoff

CHARLES SCRIBNER'S SONS · NEW YORK

7 86. 3
W 5-8 m
8 8 8 0 4
May 1974

1 3 5 7 9 11 13 15 17 19 MH/C 20 18 16 14 12 10 8 6 4 2

Printed in the United States of America
SBN: 684-10654-x (cloth)

Library of Congress Catalog Card Number: 79-85263

Contents

Foreword

❧✦❧

THIS book contains all the available manuscripts of the late Abby Whiteside. She wrote most of them after finishing *Indispensables of Piano Playing*, but we have included, for the sake of completeness, a few essays from an earlier period. The most important project, in which she planned to present the essence of her principles — especially as they had crystallized in the years after she had finished writing *Indispensables of Piano Playing* — is the study of the problems found in the Chopin Etudes.

It was completely fitting that she should choose the Etudes for her next major undertaking. Although in her work she dealt with a varied and extensive repertoire, the Chopin Etudes were at the very core of her teaching. She was convinced that Chopin, because of his affinity with the piano, had had a particularly keen awareness of the problems involved in playing it with both virtuosity and beauty. When she decided that neither the traditional nor any other current teaching had provided working solutions for the obstacles which even talented students sometimes meet, answers for achieving expert playing, and, for that matter, even defining what was the basis of piano mastery, her first step was to learn to play all of the Chopin Etudes with speed and ease.

She never changed, nor had any reason to change, her opinion that anyone who could play all of these Etudes well would be equipped to handle any technical demands that he might encounter. Therefore, every student was encouraged by her to study one Etude after another. Some of her most significant discoveries were made while she was trying to solve problems which these Etudes posed to various pupils.

Her own musical training and general education had been of a fairly conventional nature. We know of nothing there that could have been responsible for so firing up her imagination or arousing her curiosity; she must have been born with the restless and relentlessly inquiring mind which ultimately led her so far from the concepts which are still widely and unquestioningly accepted by pianists and piano teachers. She was born in 1881 in Vermillion, South Dakota. After completing her public school education she enrolled at the University of South Dakota where she majored in music and graduated with highest honors. Having taught for several years at the University of Oregon, she went, in 1908, to Germany, where she studied with Rudolf Ganz. After her return to the United States, she settled in Portland, Oregon and became a very successful teacher. Nevertheless, because she needed a wider scope for her teaching, she moved to New York in 1923 and started all over again.

She lived and taught there for the rest of her life. During summers, however, from 1922 to 1956, she taught in Chicago, Dallas, Portland, San Francisco, and Los Angeles. She became known in Los Angeles through the efforts of Carolyn Alchin, the author of *Applied Harmony*, who had achieved a position of considerable eminence among educators, at first on the West Coast and ultimately on a nation-wide scale. Having become interested in Abby Whiteside's principles of teaching piano, Carolyn Alchin invited her to come to Los Angeles and urged her students in harmony and composition to study piano with her. Abby Whiteside also lectured and taught at several universities: New York University, University of Chicago, Eastman School of Music, and Mills College.

It was at some point in the early Twenties that her mounting dissatisfaction with the techniques she had learned from her teachers culminated in a resolve to find new answers and new techniques. In her preface to *Indispensables of Piano Playing* (written approximately in 1948) she wrote: "Teaching has been an exciting experience since I squarely faced the unpleasant fact, more than twenty-five years ago, that the pupils in my studio played or didn't play, and that was that. The talented ones progressed, the others didn't — and I could do nothing about it." Once started, this search never stopped; it was difficult, full of zigzags, and required remarkable tenacity. She was a dedicated teacher, and nothing was more important to her than her teaching. She was a perfectionist, never content for long with anything that merely worked reasonably well. One of her lifelong convictions was that the fundamental way of learning, of achieving piano mastery, was the same for the very gifted, the less gifted, and even ungifted students. There was not a totally different way for each. If a suggested coordination was close enough to the truth, the gifted would bridge the gap, but the less gifted might very well be hampered. As a result, she discarded any diagnosis, no matter how effective it was with some students, if it did not consistently help all of them to improve — within the limits of their own potential — their performance. It was not enough for her to be close; she had to be absolutely right. Then again, as some new principle she was applying would sharpen her listening and diagnosing, she would notice defects in the results produced by this very principle and would seek to modify the thing which had improved her teaching.

She studied anatomy so that her inborn talent for analyzing what the performer did would be strengthened by this knowledge. Watching closely the performance of great instrumentalists, dancers, jazz pianists, athletes — anyone with any kind of physical skill — became a life-long occupation. (For example: She found a solution for teaching octaves after watching a drummer who accompanied the Hindu dancer, Shankar.) And, of course, she was constantly testing her various discoveries on pupils and modifying her theories on the basis of the results.

We thought that at least an outline of the multitude of changes in her teaching — some imperceptible, others momentous — should be presented here, partly because we are convinced that we are dealing with the concepts of an original and profound mind, and partly because some acquaintance with the procedures she used in her explorations and some of the more important changes she had made in the past would give the reader a better perspective for evaluating her ultimate conclusions as stated in this book. Her concepts, innovationary and pioneering as they are, could be of crucial importance in the teaching of performance. And they do differ from all other teaching in the sense that all other approaches when dealing with the physical action of playing concentrate on articulation — the production of individual tones; there is nothing which deals with the physical production of a phrase.

Abby Whiteside's work on the control of playing by the upper arm helped her to discover that the physical continuity which the upper arm exerts through its pull is not only the basis of speed without strain, it is also the essential physical counterpart of musical continuity — the continuity within the phrase, and in the phrase-to-phrase progression. Without it there can be no beauty in performance. This physical continuity, which she called *a basic rhythm*, is the most important factor in the creation of a beautiful performance. A sensitive, phrasewise performance will not take place — no matter how much scholarship, emotional involvement, and natural musical endowment is present — unless the performer uses this basic rhythm continuously whether he is aware of it or not. It is only when the emotional response to the aural image of the music creates in the performer's body a physical response, a basic rhythm, as a counterpart to the rhythmic flow in a composition, that he is enabled to realize to the fullest extent the beauty inherent in the music. Now, many great artists do, unconsciously, use such a rhythm. But the failure of many other performers, whose playing occasionally indicates the presence of the highest order of musical endowment, to achieve consistent beauty in performance underlines the importance of what Abby Whiteside discovered and taught. Those artists who, using a basic rhythm, achieved greatness, managed to do so in spite of what they had been taught. How much more effective would all teaching be if the use of such a basic rhythm were to be consciously and systematically taught! She was able to produce such extraordinary improvement in her students' playing; and those students who were teachers in their own right, as they became skilled in using her methods found them so effective that they could only conclude that something new and immensely important had been discovered.

There has been additional corroboration for this viewpoint. After Abby Whiteside's death in 1956, the Abby Whiteside Foundation was established which, among other activities, distributed copies of *Indispensables of Piano Playing* to several thousand libraries in the United States and throughout the world. After a while, letters began to arrive — letters written by musicians who had read this book. Not all of them were pianists; one letter was from a violist who teaches at a well-known university. All the letters contained a remarkably similar message: They had read and reread the book and were planning to read it again; this had produced new insights into performance and teaching; they were constantly finding new points of interest and stimulus. One pianist said, "I think I know the book by heart now." This rereading is by no means surprising. It underlines the inadequacy of written language in describing a physical action which, in spite of the complexity of the many muscles involved, feels completely natural and simple. The written account permits only a step-by-step, word-by-word listing of the many actions which are performed simultaneously.

A teacher can make clear what is needed not only by oral description, but, also, by what one might call physical imagery. Holding the hand, forearm, or upper arm of the student, he can sense, as the student goes through a pantomime of performing (and on occasion actual playing) whether the coordination is right — whether the hands, for instance, are alert, too limp, or too eager (in relation to the upper arm) to get to the keys. Not only can he sense this, he can more easily convey to the student what is right, and what isn't. And what is very important — everything can be done simply, directly, and with subtlety. Apart from this he has the help of his eyes and ears. An experienced teacher can diagnose, by listening to the performance, whether a basic rhythm is operating, or whether, for example, the performance is too notewise, and whether this is due to the fingers being overactive or to some other cause. An action which in the reading will appear to be complicated and full of details can, and should, in reality, be sensed as a simple and balanced activity.

Under the circumstances several readings of a given passage in this text are really essential. Further, one must always be watchful for a possible misinterpretation, because there isn't the corroboration of motor awareness. Practicing habits do establish long-lasting associations in the mind of the musician. Reading a description of a performance, the reader who has been concerned with the actions of articulation in his practicing would find it almost inconceivable that the actions which he primarily associates with hand and fingers could be predominantly related to the upper arm. Yet, with all these difficulties, the letters did indicate that the writers had glimpsed exciting, new possibilities. As one teacher said, "I don't know if I do just what Abby Whiteside suggested, but it gets good results, and that can't be bad." Obviously, the text arouses the imagination of the readers so that new paths, new ways of handling problems are envisaged.

At first all she wanted to find out was how to achieve

speed without strain. To this day many pianists accept fatigue and pain in the forearm, hand, and fingers as an inevitable corollary of speed. Another common notion holds that if many months and even years of long, daily practice produce poor results in speed and ease there can be only one reason — lack of talent. The reality is that practicing a faulty coordination can also be responsible for this disheartening experience. Abby Whiteside's work proves it, because she found a different and effective solution which time and again worked with students who had become completely discouraged after studying with more traditional teachers. Let the student be taught that he needs "strong and independent fingers, and a steel-like wrist" and from then on, all too often, his musical goose is cooked! Even worse, that faulty coordination is the one naturally induced by the mechanics of tone production in the piano (the vertical action of the key to produce tone). The right coordination for beauty and speed is not the one most easily and naturally found by the student. The frustration can be so complete that even the most gifted students turn away in disappointment.

It is obvious that the muscles which move the upper arm and forearm are much bigger and stronger than the muscles which move the fingers. A number of teachers, aware of this, have tried to incorporate the use of the two levers into piano playing. There can be a world of difference in the way the two interact, and there is a good deal of difference in the analysis by these teachers.

Abby Whiteside, herself, went through a number of significant changes in the analysis of just what does happen. The first stage was the recognition that the upper arm must, to use her own words, "run the show." The muscles which move the upper arm are in the torso, and from the earliest stages she was concerned with the shoulder joint, where the upper arm, so to say, draws its power. At that time she thought that all that the forearm, hand, and fingers did was to function as bony, alert extensions of the upper arm whose power they transmitted.

Aside from that, the student did not need to concern himself with the action at the wrist, hand, or fingers. Nature — the instinctive coordination of the body — would provide whatever had to be done. For instance, she felt that the rotary action of the forearm would "take care of itself." Thinking about it, or trying to do something about it would cause it to be bigger than was desirable.

She presented this analysis in her first book, *The Pianist's Mechanism*, published by G. Schirmer in 1929. To illustrate the constant changes she made in her teaching in a search for perfection, when a new student asked, at the end of 1931, whether he should buy this book, she answered, "Don't bother; it's out of date." She continued firm in the belief that the upper arm must be a prime factor in the coordination for playing, but the manner of applying control by the upper arm was modified repeatedly and, at times, drastically in the following twenty-five years. Even then she believed that imagery was much more important in transferring the desired coordination to the student than a prosaic listing of the various factors of this coordination. Above all, she was always a teacher and was as much concerned with the means for communicating an analysis to a pupil as with the analysis itself. For example, in the early Thirties she had read and very much approved of Otto Ortmann's book, *The Physiological Mechanics of Piano Technique*. Commenting many years later, almost at the end of her career, she said, "I am still convinced that his analysis of what happens when one plays well is accurate. My question is, how would he teach it?"

Sometime in the early Thirties, she began to explore the possibility of the torso governing a pianist's performance by a gentle but continuous pushing. The strongest emotional and physical response to music takes place in the torso; the muscles which move the upper arms are also in the torso. How very natural then if the upper arms which, according to this analysis, dominate all the activity of the forearms, hands, and fingers were, in their turn, to be dominated by this continuous, gentle action of the torso. Now, many pianists who have been trained to use a finger technique primarily, also sway and weave while playing the piano. This physical action does *not* always affect finding and striking the keys; pushing had to be involved in the very actions of performance if it were to have a significant effect.

An essential factor of musical playing had, for the first time, been uncovered: There is a physical basis not only for virtuosity but for continuity and beauty in performance. She began to notice that the great artists did, in fact, when carefully observed, reveal such a basis, whether they were aware of it or not. For her, careful observation of the artists meant watching particularly how they used their arms and torsos rather than just their fingers and possibly wrists. It is important to note that the same physical coordination which produces speed and brilliance produces continuity and beauty as well.

She began to call this coordination a *basic rhythm*, and sometimes just *rhythm*.* When she used that word she was never referring to the time-values of notes or to the meter of the music. One needs to dip only slightly into the writings of musicians about the word *rhythm* to realize how much vagueness and contradiction there is about the meaning of the word. Yet, curiously, there is unanimity about the pertinence of the word in dealing with all phases of music making. Under these circumstances it is only important that the author's intended meaning should not be misread. She did not so much classify the elements of music which were to be placed under the heading of rhythm but, rather, explored painstakingly all the nuances of physical response to the aural image which produced the flow of sound within the structure of a phrase and in the phrase-to-phrase sequence. The rhythm in the music she called a rhythm of form. The torso initiated and implemented in the pianist this basic rhythm which was his response to the music.

* See Glossary.

This phase lasted for several years, until Abby White-side came to a momentous decision. The torso would control a performance more effectively if it initiated a basic rhythm by a gentle pull — instead of pushing! At this stage she began to achieve remarkable transformations in the playing of her students. She became increasingly concerned with the continuity of activity in-between the striking of keys, because musical continuity was to be achieved by the kind of activity that took place between articulations. To achieve what she then called a *rocking rhythm* she had the students sway, at first with exaggeration, then more and more snugly. She had them bounce, while playing, in an action not very different from the equestrian's posting.

Another device to make the torso directly active in playing was the torso stroke. She had, for many years, used what she called a *full-arm stroke** to activate the upper arm which moved in an extravagant arc so that it was the instigator of the action for finding and striking keys; the forearm, hand, and fingers, by staying alert and not moving independently of the upper arm, served to transmit the power of the upper arm. This time it was the torso which acted as the power source, the upper arm as an alerted extension of the torso. The tonal pattern for the full-arm stroke was used,† but with one change: The pianist had to start with an octave skip. Wider lateral distances were needed for the torso.

Both hands in double octaves.

The torso, by hunching over, would bring the arms down so that the double octaves were struck, and then, by

* See Glossary.
† See Ex. No. 17.

straightening up, the torso raised the arms and moved to the next octaves. The lateral distance was covered by the lateral swaying of the torso.

To the reader this might seem to be a somewhat outlandish form of practicing. But, once the student managed to keep the arms from moving independently of the torso, the motion by the torso to find and strike the keys was neither awkward nor laborious and did serve to alert it. Using these devices or — a favorite word of hers — gadgets, several other students achieved a transformation in their playing that seemed little short of miraculous.

In spite of this, she announced one day that it was the upper arms, and not the torso, which could best initiate and implement a basic rhythm by a gentle pull. To a student who remonstrated she said: "Yes, you learned to play with a rhythm using the torso, but I found that this approach didn't work well with some students. Therefore it isn't completely right." She used the following example to illustrate one of the reasons for her change: If one, so to say, locked the arms with the torso and swung from side to side, it would feel considerably more awkward than if the arms, in their lateral swing, were free, and the torso snug and following the arm activity instead of initiating it.

Essentially, this was her final analysis. It does not mean there were no further modifications. For instance, sometime later she said that she still felt that the arms were the initiators of a rhythm, but the torso must be alert and responsive; otherwise a truly vital, emotionally involved rhythm would not be achieved by the performer.

Another change came in the teaching of *alternating action*.* For years Abby Whiteside had been so concerned with transferring the main burden of playing to the upper arms that for a long time it seemed to her that the primary function of the forearms, hands, and fingers was simply to transmit the power of the upper arms. If they

* See Glossary.

stayed alert, as bony extensions of the upper arms, nature would do the rest. There came a time when she saw that the forearms and hands could work — not independently of the upper arms, but under a "canopy of the pulling activity of the upper arms" — and this would result in a more supple and efficient coordination for playing. She was impressed by the realization that there would be no wasted actions — motions unproductive of sound (away from the keys, instead of towards them). There was an interplay between the forearm and hand in striking the keys: When the forearm was flexed the hand was thrown down into tone (high wrist), then, the forearm was extended, raising the hand (low wrist), once again producing tone — the hand and fingers being used as alert levers for transferring and delivering the power of the upper arm and forearm, and never operating independently to find and strike the keys. But, this entire activity was always supervised, dominated, controlled by the pull of the upper arm. *The control of all other actions by the upper-arm pull is the keystone of her final analysis, from which, once arrived at, she never deviated in her teaching.* There is a particularly good illustration of alternating action in the analysis of the Chopin Etude, Op. 10, No. 7. At a later stage the alternating action became refined into a kind of flutter of the hand being shaken by the forearm and upper arm when the Etude was played at top speed.

This very sketchy outline of the twenty-five-year evolution of Abby Whiteside's teaching bears very much on the problem that we faced when we undertook to prepare these manuscripts for publication. Our first, subjective desire was to preserve every word and to change nothing of what she had written. Yet, at the same time, objective judgment told us that it was impossible to do so. The manuscripts were in somewhat rough shape. They were neither complete nor polished. There were two versions of the introductory chapter to *Mastering the Chopin Etudes*. We found some discrepancies between the various manuscripts and, in some cases, between what she had written and, according to our recollection, what she had taught at lessons. For example: She wrote (page 56), "The aural image should be established and accurate before the outlining begins." Because the subject of outlining is discussed in detail in the text and glossary, it is enough at this point just to say that afterwards she came to the conclusion that the aural image could and should be learned from the very beginning (i.e. before the music is known) by outlining in the tempo indicated by the composer. Another example: When she started teaching outlining she recommended a simple and rather orderly procedure, such as playing the first note (or chord) in each measure; later on, she felt that outlining — or pulsing, as she called it at times — must be more spontaneous, varied, and altogether unpredictable, even to the performer himself, if an emotional rhythm was to be stimulated by it.

A particularly important discrepancy is found in *Practicing a Performance*, on page 142. We could not date this article precisely. It was in a notebook where other entries were dated 1953. This matter of dates is relevant because both of us continued to study with her to the end of her stay in New York (1956). The suggestion that, while "the upper arm continues in propelling its power into key in any direction that becomes useful as it utilizes the time element between tones etc." (with its implication that the upper arm does not always pull) never found its way into her lessons. We recall distinctly, and at least one set of notes by another of Abby Whiteside's students duplicates our own memories: She stressed that the pull at the shoulder joint can be maintained even as the upper arm comes forward. This is a very important point. Basic to her later teaching was the precept that the upper arm actively participates in the entire performance at the piano by a pull. From this standpoint no action or articulation is taken with just the forearm, hand, or fingers acting alone; the upper arm always plays an important role in every action which produces tone.

This is essential because only the upper arm, in Abby Whiteside's analysis, is capable of controlling horizontal activity, because of the structure of the shoulder joint. Another indication that this was the analysis she planned to present is a pencilled note next to a passage in one of her notebooks, which described the action of the forearm extension (page 51); she had written, "better relate this to the upper arm." Whether the statement found on page 142 was a fleeting idea which she had given up or had never developed, we did think that it had to be included, but we also felt the need of stating our own position about it.

Our decision about completing any of her writings, or making any major changes was governed by our consciousness of the importance of her principles, and by one other consideration. We wanted the many persons who had studied with Abby Whiteside or had become interested in her work after reading her previous book to be quite certain that what they read was essentially her text. Where we were obliged to make any changes or additions, we made sure that the reader was informed that the text was ours. We made as few changes as possible. In essence, we tried to avoid any important alteration of the sense of what she had written. We also avoided, with just a few exceptions, writing extensive additions to her text. We thought that such extensive elaboration would be fair neither to her nor to us. Therefore we decided not to finish her manuscript about the Chopin Etudes. Because we wanted to preserve every bit of her writing, we included both versions of the Introduction to *Mastering the Chopin Etudes*. We thought that pointing out the occasional discrepancies between what she had written and what we remembered of our lessons with her would help to define more accurately what she taught. We have every reason for believing that the discrepancies do exist only because these were preliminary drafts. Using the same reasoning, when we found some differences between the various manuscripts we thought it would be useful to indicate which version was closer to what we recalled. Even these differences in formulation could be stimulating to pianists and teachers who are also searching for satisfactory answers to problems of performance.

With all our self-imposed restrictions, there still was much that had to be done. In the summer of 1952, Abby Whiteside went to Florence, Italy for the express purpose of working intensively on the Chopin Etudes. Her notebooks for that period contain a good deal of material which could be used with little or no changes. But after that she was plagued by illness and, because she loved teaching so much, when a choice had to be made between teaching and writing, she always chose to teach. Therefore, the writing from that period was somewhat rough, consisting of hastily jotted-down thoughts which were to be expanded, organized, and incorporated into the final version. Or, there were longer drafts in which she had been concerned with putting down the general, overall thought, leaving the corrections, particularizations, and organization of material to a later time, which unfortunately never came.

In our editing we responded to the needs of the manuscript. Where a sentence was hazy or disjointed, we rewrote it, always taking care to leave the intended sense. From a mass of isolated notes we selected those remarks, which, though they remained isolated, contained observations which we thought would amplify and clarify her principles, or show a useful application to piano practice (pp. 128-136 and 145-150.)

In some cases, e.g. the second version of the Introduction, pp. 108-127, the contents had to be regrouped for an easier reading sequence. In Etude, Op. 10, No. 7 she had not written out the musical examples she referred to. It was a comparatively simple matter for us, knowing how she taught the alternating action used in this Etude, to decide just what examples she had in mind.

She clearly had intended to write a detailed analysis

of the practicing procedure for the ninth measure of Etude, Op. 25, No. 10. Because she had written out the essential general analysis, and as long as the reader was put on notice that the description of practicing procedure was ours, it seemed desirable to add this section (pp. 73-78). The same circumstances existed in the case of Etude, Op. 25, No. 11; therefore we wrote out the detailed practicing procedure on pages 105 to 107.

The Glossary, pp. 188-200, was entirely our work. It was Abby Whiteside's custom, both in teaching and writing, to find some word or phrase to describe various facets of performance. She did this in order to present her ideas more vividly and succinctly. Because she often gave these words a special meaning, one differing from the generally accepted sense, we thought that a Glossary would be useful to the reader. In some cases, where defining a term did not seem sufficient, we went into the details of practicing procedure.

This volume and the previous book complement each other. The contents of *Mastering the Chopin Etudes and Other Essays* reflect the author's thinking in her last years, during which she reached the greatest skill and subtlety in teaching the use of a basic rhythm for learning to play the piano with all the brilliance and supple continuity that native endowment allows; but *Indispensables of Piano Playing* represents the most comprehensive statement by her of the principles she discovered. It seems to us that a careful study of the two will clarify and amplify for the reader the essence of what Abby Whiteside taught.

*   *   *

Just as the principles which Abby Whiteside evolved diverged extensively from the mainstream of present-day teaching, so did she differ from other teachers in the very procedure of giving a lesson. She was completely certain of the importance of what she was uncovering and took care to write down — sometimes sketchily, at other times in detail — the various stages of her evolving principles and the effectiveness of some new device. But, although she was always aware of the importance of skill and finesse in the application of her principles, she did not describe in sufficient detail how she herself taught. Therefore some mention of this seems very much to the point.

A lesson — every lesson — was, for her, an exciting and creative experience. She never was casual about a lesson; it was never a routine procedure. She wanted to and did approach it in the same manner as one would a concert by some new and gifted performer. This was true whether the student was talented or not. She, therefore, trained herself to "wipe the slate clean" as she called it. She listened for enjoyment — not for errors; when something in the performance interfered with this she tried to find out what the fault was. What she didn't want to do was to listen to see if such and such mistake, made at the last lesson, had now been corrected. She once said that she always had a general idea of the stage the student had reached, but, otherwise, she did not want to remember in detail just how he had performed a given composition the previous week.

Nor was it her practice merely to reiterate what she had said at the previous lesson. After all, if a creative diagnosis was to be made she felt that she had to listen to every performance as if it were a fresh experience. So, in trying to solve a problem she was just as likely as not to come up with something completely new. Frequently the solution would be astonishingly simple. On occasion, when she was particularly pleased with the result of the new device she would exclaim indignantly, "Now why couldn't I have thought of that before?"

Because of what she was striving for, the very nature, the content of her lessons differed from what one customarily expects. A lesson was a fundamental opportunity to transfer to the student the awareness of how it felt to play with a rhythm. For this purpose she used imagery, physical handling, and anything which suggested itself to her. We dropped our hands, and gently picked them up in order to realize how we could have alert wrists with a minimum exertion of energy. We twirled knobs — imaginary and real — to get an active rotary action and general aliveness of the arms. We snapped imaginary whips to learn how the upper arm controlled the actions of the forearm and hand. We held lightly a piece of paper or imagined holding a baby bird to make the palm alive for playing — transmitting the power of the arm. This meant that the student could learn something at a lesson which improved his playing even if he had not practiced all week.

The lesson was never merely an examination to find out how much the student had progressed by dint of practicing. In conventional teaching nothing very constructive can be done at a lesson about a student's performance if he has not practiced. We are not suggesting that practicing is unnecessary for the learning of a composition. But that there could be a significant improvement in the playing of a new and unfamiliar piece as a result of what had been done at a lesson is a clear indication of an important qualitative difference in the nature of the teaching process which was employed.

Perhaps it is also characteristic of the way she taught that there was no insistence that the student accept her idea of what the right tempo should be. It is understood that we are not talking about playing an Adagio at top speed, or a fast piece at a creeping pace. Beyond indicating that she herself preferred a different speed, she permitted the student, when he was very sure of his preference, to follow his own choice of speeds. She did no coaching. But, when her listening for musical enjoyment was interrupted by notewise playing, or for any other reason which made the student play without a subtle and pliant continuity, she would immediately stop him so that they could work on the problem. She would be apologetic about the interruption but was certain that a fault would be easier to correct if one worked at it while the impression was fresh. Sometimes, when there was a particularly stubborn problem — usually one which resisted diagnosis — there would be a stop at the same place week after week. But she never lost her temper over this, no matter how long it persisted, so long as the student followed all her suggestions.

She always tried to be brief and to the point. She explained that she had always been irritated by those of her own teachers who would expound at length and in great detail some obvious point, or, at any rate, a point which was obvious to her. If the student wanted, or needed, additional elaboration she provided it with no irritation or impatience. Although every student knew the general theory behind her teaching, he did not necessarily know all the devices she used. Because her devices, or gadgets — as she liked to call them — were invented on the spot to solve a given problem, they were not always volunteered when such a problem did not exist: That would clutter up a lesson unnecessarily.

Her standards for the teaching profession were uncompromisingly high and at times surprising. For instance, while discussing the teaching of children she once said: "If a child of average intelligence, average musical equipment, and an average coordination does not have, after studying for a while, a sense of accomplishment and an interest in music and the piano, it is *always* the fault of the teacher and never the fault of the child."

Certainly one of her most important techniques was the use of physical sensation to transfer to the student the awareness of just how the correct performance felt. Holding the student's hand, for example, as she tried to make him alert or pantomime a performance, she could both sense the slightest sluggishness or an eagerness in the hand or fingers (instead of the upper arm) to find tone and, in turn, make him aware of this.

To use a homely example, one bite of a tart, green apple is worth thousands of words if one wishes to show someone just how a green apple tastes. Even in actual performance she could, by touching his elbow, forearm, or hand, without interfering with the playing, make the student notice when his hands or fingers were more active than his upper arms in finding the keys. This involved considerable finesse, which posed no problem for her. She was endowed with remarkable physical deftness and all her life sought to achieve even more, because to her this deftness was essential for expert teaching.

It is pertinent at this point to quote her on the subject of coaching. She had serious reservations about its value because she thought that coaching could not possibly do anything except touch the surface of a musician's playing habits. It was only teaching, she thought, that could reach deep down to find the fundamental physical causes for inadequacies in a performance and do something about it which was constructive and lasting.

She constantly stressed the necessity of being emotionally involved in practicing a performance. Early in her career she learned that the human body is so constituted that the physical coordination used when one is emotionally involved in a performance is different from the one operating when one is not. This, incidentally, is the reason why the knowledge of which bones are moved by which muscles is, by itself, of comparatively little value to the pianist or teacher. Because she was searching for the basis of a beautiful performance, it was clear to her that an automatic, uninvolved performance — unfortunately, a commonplace state for the musician practicing exercises — is not merely negative, it is an actively harmful experience. An essential element of a superlative performance is systematically ignored, avoided. The ultimate result of automatic, uninspired practicing can only be an automatic, uninspired performance.

It was no accident that none of her devices were called "exercises." They were called "gadgets," "set-ups." They were used to establish the total physical and emotional basis for a beautiful and authoritative performance. This was not a subjective dislike of a word. A word sets up a response. An exercise is a chore, a routine drill. Its objective result can only be bad. If a full-arm stroke was to be played, it had to be "a thing of beauty in itself." Not only were the notes of the full-arm stroke to be endowed with the sense of being beautiful, but, particularly, the motion of the arms was to be sensed and performed as if that motion was intrinsically beautiful. An outline had to engross the performer in every way if it was to produce an "emotionally-involved basic rhythm," which would enable the pianist to say what he had to say. If he couldn't practice an outline that way it would be much better not to practice it at all.

She was vitally concerned with the ear's role in performance. She once said that if one had to state as briefly as possible the basis of beautiful performance one could say: ear and coordination. She was quite concerned with ear training, but ear training aimed in a specific direction: having the performer's ear function at its peak capacity *during* performance. General ear training such as singing intervals or working at musical dictation has a value for the student, but it isn't specific enough to assure good auditory habits for the performer. Even talented performers do not necessarily have the ear dominate the playing at all times.

Learning a musical composition involves the ears, eyes, muscular motor sense, as well as the mind. Because music deals with sound, Abby Whiteside thought the ear must be predominant. She considered that stressing the importance of reading in the early stages of studying music was faulty and productive of enduring harmful effects, and recommended that teaching to read be postponed for as long as possible. Instead, to encourage and nurture good listening habits, she advised that pieces be taught by rote, and that students transpose learned pieces. This kind of practicing was the best way to ensure that the ear was always in command of the playing.

However, it must be stressed that she did not think the ear could, by itself, either establish good physical habits or correct bad ones.

A musician's ear is conditioned by his practicing habits — it is not some objective gauge which hears accurately what is happening, no matter what the training has been. Notewise practicing develops notewise listening. Notewise practicing does not just refer to practicing slowly, so that each note and chord of the composition is singled out for attention, nor to frequent stopping to correct mistakes. Even musicians who customarily become acquainted with a new composition by playing it through at full speed in order to get an over-all impression can still, and quite unintentionally, be nurturing note-by-note listening. Predominant concern with hands, fingers, and forearms — levers which are constructed by nature so that they function vertically and can, therefore, be involved only in articulation of individual notes — will result in a playing where the individual articulation of each successive note or chord is most important, and an ear which listens notewise.

Training the ear to listen phrasewise or, as Abby Whiteside would say, "with a rhythm," calls for establishing an involvement with the upper arm — specifically with the pull exerted by the upper arm — because the circular joint by which it is connected with the torso enables the arm to control horizontal progression — the progression *between* the notes of the phrase.

To establish such a coordination a student must become keenly aware of how different actions feel in his own body. This is not a matter of large and obvious differences. There are nuances involved; these physical nuances can be felt; they cannot be heard. Although the muscles involved are many, and the coordination therefore complex, it is easy to sense even subtle nuances once one has learned to be physically aware. Where the problem involves getting rid of faulty physical habits — habits which prevent speed and continuity — and installing new ones, we are faced with an even more insistent need of having the student cultivate this perception of physical sensation if he is to be successful. This is by no means easy. In the first place, students ordinarily are not trained or accustomed to being acutely aware of physical actions. In the second place, they frequently don't even want to, although they are sometimes conscious of the need to change their way of playing.

The ear by itself will not make the student conscious of what he is doing that is wrong. The fact is, the student who is accustomed to notewise listening will not always hear the subtleties of dynamics and timing which are involved, and when, on rare occasions, he does hear them he will not always prefer the superior, more continuous performance. The notes seem to go by too fast, in too bland a fashion. He wants to stop and listen to each note in turn.

But, for Abby Whiteside, the results of her teaching, the extent to which the new coordination had indeed become habitual could best be measured by what the student did at a performance — especially a public performance — with his ears controlling that performance. She knew and spoke frequently of the great aural endowment a student had to have before he could even consider a professional career as a performer.

Improvisation was another of her prime tools. It was used with two goals in mind: involving the ear and creating a basic rhythm in the student. The most untalented student can learn to improvise, in the same sense that even a person of limited intelligence and education can speak in sentences rather than unrelated words. Whether or not the pianist is gifted, the improvisation will still tend to progress phrasewise. The improviser does not strike one note and then stop to decide what note to play next. From the standpoint of the ear, improvisation establishes the most immediate relationship between what the ear images and the playing mechanism performs. Therefore, she would use improvisation to establish in the student the habit of a phrase-to-phrase progression both physically and aurally. Then, this activity would be transferred to a composition which the student was learning. The results were at times astonishing.

One procedure which she occasionally used with great success really seemed quite uncanny. When she couldn't readily diagnose what was wrong she would sit down at the piano and imitate the student's performance. She sought to identify with him for the moment so that she felt and acted as he had. This seemed to give her a sense of what he had done. At times, the moment she sat down at the piano, even before she had touched a key she would announce, "I know what's wrong." The proof, of course, lies in the fact that when the student made an adjustment in response to her criticism his playing improved. This was such a feat of virtuosity in diagnosis, so impressive. Once, a very gifted student, but something of a wag, exclaimed, "Abby! If you had done this in Salem, Mass., in Colonial Times, they would have burned you for a witch!" Needless to say, she glowed — with pleasure.

The first lesson with a new student was a momentous occasion for her. She geared herself emotionally for it as for a debut. The problem was to bring him somehow into a totally new world of ease and continuity. Once, when asked what she did at such a lesson, she answered, "A hundred and one things. We play a scrap of this and a scrap of that. A hundred times I grasp his hand, or arm, or forearm to give him some sensation of what I want him to feel."

A certain physical coordination was aimed at. Whether the student was a comparative beginner or an advanced professional pianist, such a coordination could be established most easily after he had become attuned to sensing keenly what was happening physically. To her, that was of the first order of importance. For example, when she discussed a pupil who had learned to use a basic rhythm in playing, she said: "He has a basic rhythm and knows how it feels." Therefore, using all the treasure-trove of gadgets that the years of teaching had accumulated, she sought to evoke a meaningful awareness in the student of the physical sensation of playing with a rhythm.

*   *
*

We wish to thank all those who have helped us to prepare this book for publication.

Eunice Nemeth and Robert Helps sent us notes they had kept of their lessons with Abby Whiteside.

Roger Boardman made available to us his dissertation, *A History of Theories of Teaching Piano Technic.*

Willia Wight and Carolyn Haughton made available for inclusion in this book the article, *Flaws in Traditional Teaching of Piano,* which had been presented to them, in manuscript form, by Abby Whiteside.

Marion Flagg, Mary M. Champlin, and Stanley Baron, after reading the original manuscripts, made many valuable suggestions.

We also wish to thank Jean Prostakoff and Noah Rosoff for their interest and encouragement.

JOSEPH PROSTAKOFF   SOPHIA ROSOFF

Mastering the Chopin Etudes
June, 1952

❧❦❧

No ONE knows all the facts involved — the subtleties
in the balance of activity of all the muscles used in playing the piano — but the principle used in learning this
coordination is not different from the one in constant
use in our daily living: We want to do something, and
nature automatically helps us to do it.

We must constantly keep in mind the realization that
nature is far more skilled at the doing than we are capable of analyzing all the intricacies of that doing. We
must remember that a coordination made in nature's
way is never a coordination that is put together after
all the parts have been practiced separately. From the
very beginning, nature uses the mechanism as a whole
in response to the desire to achieve a result. Observe
the eating process: We want food, and that desire, alone,
creates the action which feeds us. It is the same whether
it is a baby learning to eat, or an adult cooking a meal
and eating it. In this entire process we pay attention
only to the results desired; it does not occur to anyone to
bother with the manner in which each movement is made.

The difference between learning to play the Chopin
Etudes and feeding oneself is that the process for playing is
more intricate and demands a musical talent. This talent,
among other things, implies a pitch perception which is
so accurate that a body can move accurately to produce
the tones which the ear has imaged and wants to hear.

26

Does this mean that without perfect pitch no one can learn to play the Etudes? No. It simply means that the person without perfect pitch will not learn them so easily, and that there will not be the same security in performance after they are learned as when perfect pitch is a part of the natural endowment.

Only an accurate control can give a specific command. For the musician who deals with sound, perfect pitch is that accurate control. We do not fumble in judging the distance of a curb. The eye is a perfect control and gauges the distance accurately; the body automatically responds, and we step up at the exact moment for landing accurately. Perfect pitch is the perfect control for *automatically* landing on the right key when making music.

Perfect pitch, by itself, is not the only requirement; it could lead to a notewise playing. All too frequently we hear accuracy without real beauty in performance. All such playing lacks a basic rhythm. A sensitive, strong basic rhythm — the only action which can prevent perfect pitch from settling into a notewise procedure — is the superlative coordinator for beautifying each phrase. Playing may not be creative even with a basic rhythm, but it can never be ugly when a rhythm is coursing on its way.

More than any other factor, this basic rhythm is the illuminating guide to the subtle beauties of great music. It is through a heightened sense of the elasticity in music that great beauty emerges in playing, and this can never happen without a basic rhythm. With the growth of sensitivity to this infinitely subtle give-and-take in playing a phrase, the emotional surge will find its outlet with the physical action which produces a rhythm of phrase-playing instead of the action which produces one tone at a time.

Variation in dynamics must not be predetermined if the greatest beauty is to pour forth in a performance; nor should there be too many climaxes because the emotional surge will then find its sole outlet in the hitting process. It is only when a surging basic rhythm is the current charged with emotion that a performer develops all his resources of perception.

Here is something of the utmost importance to be learned and learned thoroughly: *For a performer all listening is conditioned by the kind of physical activity which dominates his playing.* If there is a separate initiation of power for each tone he will listen notewise, and then there will be insufficient subtlety in the use of power to create a beautiful statement. But, if tones are produced inside a current of power (e.g. glissando) he will listen in a comprehensive manner from the beginning to the end of the musical statements. This phrasewise listening is the only kind of listening which can be sufficiently creative to bring the greatest subtleties of nuance into a performance. If this crucial point concerning listening could be made a reality at the outset, there would be a clear understanding of the damage that is done to every phase of performance when the physical habits for playing details are dealt with before there is any consideration of the physical habits which deal with a basic rhythm.

It is this crucial lack of developing a technique dealing with the production of a basic rhythm which is at the root of all the problems, both musical and technical, in the Etudes.

There are innumerable approaches, traditional and otherwise, for developing a technique dealing with details; but, so far as I know, not one of them makes it imperative that details (speaking of physical actions) are second in importance to the basic rhythm. But, unless this basic rhythm is installed first, the native capacity will have been thwarted in using its magnificent equipment for a coordination which includes the whole as well as the parts.

A basic rhythm is always implemented with the fundamental power which is tone producing. For the pianist the all-powerful lever is the upper arm. It can integrate the power of lesser levers with its action if the action of the upper arm deals with a phrasewise rhythm. The upper arm is the only lever equipped to deal with a continuous rhythm. The power of the upper arm is made effective by the torso which, by being grounded, as it were, against the chair seat, acts as the arm's fulcrum. The upper arm has the connecting joint with the torso. This connecting joint is a marvel of dexterity. It allows action in all directions with continuity.

The manner in which the torso amplifies the rhythm initiated by the arm is as individual as the performer himself for the activity which will express the performer's emotional reaction to the music. Because this rhythm in the torso does express emotion (the mood of the music), there may be extravagant movements; or there may be intensity of emotion which is expressed by a steady holding of the reins of the performing tools, with very little movement for the eye to see. But there will be a vital activity, whether it be in holding, weaving about, or bouncing around (the extremes, with every modi-fication in between), and it is a pity that such activity has been labeled "mannerisms" because of a lack of understanding of the part it plays in the performer's projection of his art.

Once I taught a big talent for four years before he admitted to himself that his ears alone could not produce the results he desired. He never played with the grace he wanted until he took stock of the activity in the torso which created a basic rhythm. Then his playing began to grow in grace and charm, and beauty came into every phrase.

Rather than have the teacher be too specific as to the kind of movement to be made in initiating a rhythm, it is better for you to observe what the artist does, and what you do when a band goes by, or when you are fascinated by dance music. If you are on your feet when the band goes by you will move with the music, even if ever so slightly, unless you have learned to be an inhibited person. All the children will bob around. Watch them.

We are not so free in the sitting position as when standing, but there are two bones (ischia) which we sit against, just as we stand against our feet, and we can, in the sitting position, shift balance and do all the things in miniature to express our emotional response to music that we do habitually in a standing position.

It is true that there are many expert listeners who get their entire satisfaction and delight with simply the sound of the music. But they are not the experts who are the most successful performers. The real performers get their satisfaction with both ears and rhythm. Since the idea is to play the Etudes with beauty, grace, and facility, one must develop the habit of listening and responding with an active body. Let the music take possession of you; when you sit down to play first of all allow the aural image to have its way and create an active response in the torso. It need not be an obvious response to anyone else but for you it means an alert balance and rhythmic response.

The first link to the playing mechanism with this rhythmic torso is the upper arm, and if the basic rhythm in the torso gets into the actual performance it will be because the upper arm takes the *initiative in arriving at tone and keeps it*. Note that the upper arm does this in playing a glissando. In the Etudes, where the other levers do participate in the coverage of distance and the use of power for tone, the result to be achieved is essentially that same relationship of upper arm to tone.

If you have a well developed set of independent fingers you will not believe this. Later, either you will become convinced, or achieve it in spite of your intellectual concept of what you do (a few players do), or you will not play the Etudes with the infectious grace and beauty born of a fundamental rhythm, even if you can produce all of the tones with both speed and accuracy.

The transition from a finger control (fingers reaching for key and producing tone) to an upper-arm control is certainly not quickly nor easily accomplished, but it can be done. When it is achieved there will be a world of difference in what you hear and the ease with which your aural image is translated into tone.

Unfortunately, there is only one way to experience this change in listening and in playing. One has to wait for nature to work the miracle by achieving a coordination which puts the upper arm in control of distance and power. Words are meaningless until the new physical habits are a reality. There is no proof in advance which can be given. There is only the complete delight and relief that there can be a definite way to beauty for those who follow through until the new habits take precedence over the old ones. It was observing these changes take place in the pianists who came to study with me which gave me the impetus for this written analysis.

Watch gifted jazz players perform. Their ears and a basic rhythm are always running the show, with nature making the coordination. They did not grow up with any traditional method of finger independence, and certainly no one can sniff at their technical equipment. They fairly extend their instrument, whatever instrument it happens to be.

Habits, conditioned reflexes, are a formidable bulwark against any real change or even understanding of suggested new patterns of action by words on a printed page. The greatest help in effecting a change of habits comes from a frequent repetition of the sensation of the desired actions transferred from teacher to pupil.

To alert the upper arm to take the place of fingers in responding to the aural image is the task which comes first in achieving the desired coordination in the playing mechanism for virtuosity in playing the Etudes.

The power of the upper arm is directly effective in tone production through a pull toward the body. Remember, every action of this first lever of the arm operates through a circular joint, and, therefore, the end of the upper arm — the elbow point — moves in a segment of a circle. It has no capacity for a simple straight up-and-down movement.

Tone on the piano is produced by a vertical action of the key. There must be a down-action in the playing mechanism to put the key down to produce tone. The nearest thing to this down-action with the upper arm is a pull *toward* the torso, for the playing position at the piano puts the elbow slightly in front of the torso. Only a pull lowers this point of the elbow. This lowering action, a movement toward the torso — a pull — can put the key down and be tone-producing. To isolate the sensation of action with the upper arm, fold up the forearm (touch the shoulder with the fingers). Then, see what the action would be if you were to strike the keyboard a fortissimo blow with the elbow. This action would be like the swing of an axe in chopping wood. The swing might feel like a pull downward, for the elbow moves downward as it swings through the circular arc toward the body.

With the forearm still folded out of the way, pantomime playing two tones, for example: middle C and the C two octaves above. Note that the tip of the arm swings again in a slightly curved line in covering the two-octave distance, but when the tone is struck (in imagination) there is a clear sensation of pulling the elbow toward the torso. The louder the tone (still in imagination) the stronger will the sensation be.

Now there are two full octaves of tones between these two C's. How will the upper arm be in control at all times if we want to play a C-major scale so that the primary action of going directly from the first C to the last C will not be destroyed? (This is where a developed finger action will destroy the meaning of the words on the page.) The actions which share the primary action of the upper arm when the scale is played involve every possible action of every lever between the elbow and the finger tip. At the moment we are not involved with these multiple actions but only with the functioning of the upper arm, because it is in control of both covering the distance from C to C and furnishing the initiative in the power-production of all the tones.

Should the action of the upper arm which was involved with playing the two outside C's be dissipated and destroyed by the production of the intervening tones, then we will have killed the goose that lays the golden egg — the basic rhythm. The phrase we are dealing with is a two-octave scale. If it is to remain intact as a unit of beauty it must have a physical action as its counterpart which is intact — an action which is continuous from C to C — the same action which played the two C's originally.

The glissando quite easily has the continuous action. How to keep that continuity and articulate each tone is the problem, and it is certainly both a musical as well as a technical problem. The musical problem demands continuity from the beginning to the end of the musical idea. The technical problem demands continuity plus articulation in tone production.

Only the power of the upper arm has the important element of continuity because it is the only lever which operates through a circular joint. Thus, the upper arm must furnish a part of the power for all the tones if the tones are to be strung together as one, rhythmic, musical unit.

The very act of continuity implies no stopping and, certainly, no sticking at the bottom of the key. This upper-arm power should never brook any obstacle put in the way of its progression by another lever bogging it down. If the upper arm is adamant in its progression from C to C then all of the other levers will be forced to conform to its timing.

Nature alone can produce such expert timing as is needed, but nature can only use its capacity for expert timing when the coordination is made from center to periphery (shoulder to hand), and that means that the upper arm must take the initiative and hold it.

It is very easy for those with perfect pitch to interrupt the flow of power to listen for pitch when they are reading from the printed page. They will never interrupt that flow of tone-producing energy when they are improvising. Why? Because the act of improvising demands the finishing of the idea being created. Tones are of no value except as they complete the musical statement. The improviser has a message to deliver, which means there is a musical goal to be reached. So, the body produces the necessary continuity in rhythmic power to produce the structural whole.

An example of this happened in my studio one day when I was working with a very gifted musician. I asked him to improvise a mazurka and then play a Chopin Mazurka. The improvised mazurka was full of grace and real beauty. The Chopin Mazurka lacked these qualities. Twice he did the same thing. He knew that I was working to transfer the kind of physical activity he used in his improvisation to the reading of the Chopin Mazurka. The third time he was successful in making this transfer, and the Chopin Mazurka was completely captivating. He looked up and said, "But it went so fast I couldn't hear it."

Thus, here is one of the serious problems in reproducing the aural image. Nothing but the continuity of an infectious rhythm can turn the trick of outwitting the excellent ear which wants to hear each tone. And nothing but the upper arm of the playing mechanism can deliver this rhythm into a performance.

If by now, with the forearm folded up, you have an awareness of the activity in the upper arm — a distinct sensation of movement — place the hand on the keyboard. With the five fingers on the first five keys of the scale, use the action of the upper arm for depressing the keys (without tone so that the sensation of activity is not diverted by listening). With one greater action in the upper arm (a pull) put the five keys down simultaneously. Then have the arm balance up and down on these

five keys (still without tone), always increasing the awareness that it is the action of the upper arm which is in
charge of the key depression. The habit of using fingers
for playing usually produces a feeling of down-pressure
or heaviness in the forearm. This must be avoided if the
upper arm is to have a chance to control the playing. It
takes much care to establish new habits — the old ones
operate before you have a chance to think about them.
Remember the sensation when the forearm was folded
up. When it is lowered into the playing position, keep
it light so that it feels out of the way of the upper arm.
With this "out-of-the-way forearm" and a fresh sensation of a depression of the keys by the upper arm, suddenly
and rather violently (fortissimo) sound the five tones as
a ripped *chord*. Consciously shut out rotary action of
the forearm as much as possible; use in its place a definite pull toward the torso — a fast, strong, short pull
by the upper arm. There will be an infinitesimal amount
of roll-over with the hand. It should remain almost in
the same position as when balancing on the keys. This
is very important if there is to be an adequate technique
developed in the upper arm.

Use the upper-arm power (pull) extravagantly — fortissimo. Then observe the results: Tones were sounded
separately, though in very rapid succession; there was
only one movement registered, that of the upper arm;
one movement in the upper arm produced five tones in
a row; this one movement of the upper arm put the keys
down so far as sensation was concerned; the power for
producing tone was used at the bottom of the key
(key bed), certainly not at the top; this means that the
power of the upper arm operated at key-bed level (very
important to note); the fingers did nothing that could
be registered except furnish a bony structure for the
upper arm to play against.

Here is the clue to the relation between the upper-arm
power and the fingers when there is easy brilliance and
speed: The upper arm furnishes the impulse and power

*for tone; the fingers stand under this power and transmit
it to the key; the fingers furnish a sturdy little bone for the
big power to play against.*

In producing the ripped five tones, the control of distance — the finding of the key — has not yet been dealt with. Now is the time to drive home this fact: *The upper arm must control — gauge all distance.* The other levers extend this upper-arm control, but they *must not* initiate it. Without the control for distance localized at the center of the radius of activity — the shoulder joint — nature cannot produce its expert coordination for an easy coverage of the keyboard.

The right key must be located before the desired tone can be produced. It is a faulty control of distance — finding the key — which never allows playing to feel well oiled and easy. Reaching for the key with the fingers is practically the root of all evil in playing; and to change the habit of doing it demands the determination of a Demosthenes. No negative approach to this problem can turn the trick. There must be a daily, hourly cultivation of awareness of the activity in the upper arm until a concrete activity takes place in response to the desire to find the key which will produce the tone desired.

Practice large skips first and again fold up the forearm so that it is relieved of temptation to go ahead of the upper arm. Use imagery, do everything that a fertile brain can concoct to register the sensation when the upper arm moves, if ever so slightly, to aim at the key to be played. This aiming involves a turning of the humerus (the bone of the upper arm) in the shoulder joint. It may be an infinitesimal turning. For moderate distances it is a tiny action. Even for a large skip the action is not great, for it is the forearm coverage in coordination with the turning of the humerus which supplies a large proportion of the horizontal distance of the keyboard. But never forget for a second that it is the humerus turning in the circular joint which is the superlative steering gear. This action is so efficient, so subtle, so natural that it is difficult to become truly aware of it. There would be no need to become aware of it if the hand had not been trained to initiate actions (the worst of which is reaching for the key) for which it should never be responsible.

From center to periphery, from shoulder to finger tip, is nature's way of making an efficient coordination — a balanced activity for covering all distance.

When the control is at the center of the playing mechanism there is no distance to frighten one. When the control is at the periphery, distances are too large to be negotiated without fear of striking the wrong key.

Think of the relation of the center to the circumference of a circle as described by a compass: no distance at the center pin, and the whole distance of the circumference with the outside pin. Yet the center pin turns the outside pin.

We realize how tremendously necessary and efficient is the turning of the humerus as it acts in all directions when we learn that the forearm can move in only one plane in relation to the upper arm, and that its rotary action is limited; yet there is never any consciousness that the forearm can't put the hand in any position necessary for playing.

Multiple difficulties in playing arise when the upper arm is not sufficiently in control.

The Etudes will balk at practically every bar when there is a faulty control of distance. That distance-control must be at the shoulder joint.

Remember that "distance" implies the finding of the key, and that has to happen before the power for tone can be applied. Even for the previously mentioned ripping of the five tones the position on the keyboard was taken before any other operation took place.

Years of teaching have taught me that when the habit of reaching for the key position with the fingers has been grooved into the playing mechanism, it is the last of all bad habits to give way to a new set of controls.

Just never take it for granted that the fingers have given up. Instead, set up a "daily dozen" of thinking patterns before the hands are allowed on the keyboard. It is wise to fold the forearm out of the way while these "set-ups" are in operation, seeking awareness of the readiness of the upper arm to take over in controlling distance and power. Through this control of distance and power, the upper arm acts as a fulcrum for the forearm.

For the delivery of a blow there must be a steady, resistant force — the fulcrum — which makes the blow effective. The torso is this steady resistance — fulcrum — for the upper arm. The fulcrum-force in the torso, which is grounded against the chair seat, is the activity which produces the basic rhythm. It is the emotional response to the musical statement.

The upper arm is the fulcrum for the forearm. The fulcrum-force in the upper arm is the pull which controls the level at which tone is produced, as well as the slight turning of the humerus which controls distance.

The illustration of this fulcrum-force in the upper arm, which seems most pertinent to me, is the control of a lariat: All of the patterns which the rope is made to go through are controlled by the hand as an extension of the primary action of the upper arm, as it makes miniature turnings, plus a consistent and continuous slight pull at the shoulder joint. Tiny actions produce fantastic shapes and patterns with the loop of the rope. Tiny actions in the upper arm produce great beauty in performance. Let the arm stop this slight turning and pulling, and the rope falls to the ground.*

Let the upper arm cease to be an alert fulcrum in performance, and all the subtle beauty disappears; the music will be sheared of its basic rhythm and will lose the continuity of the upper-arm action which implements that rhythm — filters it into the playing mechanism. Continuity in action is the all-important responsibility of the upper arm — acting through a circular joint.

* Another example of the "daily dozen" referred to above. [Eds.]

A fast and powerful repeated action at the elbow (a hinge joint) plus the rotary action (a twisting and untwisting of the two bones in the forearm) are the great assets of the forearm. The action at the elbow joint operates in one plane, flexion and extension of the forearm. Though the forearm seems to move freely in all planes, it can only do so in cooperation with the upper arm. Rotary action of the forearm is an inevitable adjunct of playing the piano. It is possible for the hand to place all five fingers on the keyboard at once only because of this rotary action plus a turning of the humerus.

The rotary action will take care of itself and should not be overstressed. Any action which will take care of itself had better be let alone. If the rotary action is overemphasized it can become a menace. Too much rotary action will diminish the technical advantage of an alternating up-and-down (flexion and extension) action of the forearm at the elbow joint. It is this up-and-down action, operated by powerful muscles, which must be cultivated to the nth degree, because it has such tremendous advantages for speed.

The forearm is the connecting lever between the source of power, the upper arm, and the hand which contacts tone through the fingers. Either it operates in conjunction with the upper arm — transmits the upper-arm power to the level of tone production — or, by a faulty down-pressure, it can cut off the upper-arm power because it is nearer to the keyboard than the upper arm.

Carry the forearm as a part of the upper arm. Keep it feeling light. The habit of letting the forearm sag (due perhaps to an emphasis on relaxation) is not too easily replaced by a consistent lightness. These two large levers — upper arm and forearm — are the bulwark of the entire technique. If they are sufficiently active and cooperative, then the hand and fingers need not be overworked.

The longer I teach — and the years are many now — the more I am convinced that the wrist joint has the unique quality of being the joint for *transmitting* action, rather than for producing a positive action. It does not put the hand up or down, but allows the up-and-down action of the forearm to flip the hand into the desired position on the keyboard.

Always there must be a down-action for producing tone; when the key goes down the tone is sounded. Why have we believed all these years that because the fingers contact the key they must put the key down? They operate with astonishing skill quite naturally when all that is asked of them is to furnish their bones for the power of the two large levers to play against. Note the brilliance and ease of the ripped chord: The fingers furnish their bony structure without any hint of putting the key down by their own initiative.

The relationship of power to finger action can be maintained, but there must be one hundred percent cooperation between the upper arm, forearm, and hand. While the upper arm is functioning as a fulcrum through a continuous pull it dominates whatever down-action of forearm or hand is needed for connecting up with tone.

There is a wonderful arrangement whereby when the forearm is coming up, the hand can be going down; and when the forearm goes down it can take the key-drop against the fingers, even though the hand goes up in relation to the end of the forearm. The hand itself tips up while the forearm goes down. In other words, this action produces a low wrist, just as flexion of the forearm and the hand going down produce a high wrist. *But*, it is the up-and-down action from the elbow joint which is furnishing the positive action in both instances, inside the pull of the upper arm. The down-action puts the key down — takes key-drop. The up-action drops the hand, while the pull of the upper arm becomes positive as the hand goes down.

The alternation between the hand and forearm, and the alternation between the positive pull in the upper arm when the hand drops into position, and the positive action of forearm when it takes the key-drop, are miracles of efficiency, *if* the wrist allows the actions of the two big levers to get through, and the fingers do not interfere by reaching for the key.

The hand moves through the wrist joint — a complicated joint which allows a free and large up-and-down action and a limited action in all directions. When the rotary action of the forearm acts in conjunction with the hand movements there is a feeling of freedom in the motion of the hand in all directions.

Restrict the rotary action temporarily and describe circles with the hand — circles from left to right and from right to left. Learn the hand movements thoroughly. Particularly note the play in the lateral action. This lateral action is not very large, but it is very important for easy arpeggios and scales. This lateral action of the hand can extend the range of the forearm action of flexion and extension.

While there can be no isolation of combinations of actions in actual playing, and no effort should be made to establish isolated actions, there are certain combinations of actions which it is very wise to be aware of in order to combat faulty habits. One of these combinations is the manner in which a quick flexion or extension of the forearm can produce a lateral action of the hand. Naturally, this will not and cannot happen unless the hand is delicately and lightly balanced as an extension of the forearm. The hand should never be strongly held in position, but, instead, so lightly that it will practically quiver like a leaf on a stem, when the forearm (the stem) moves quickly.

Place the forearm and hand (palm down) on a table, barely touching the surface. Then flex and extend the forearm in an alert, quick action which will move the hand laterally while the same light contact with the table surface is maintained.* One need not worry about the rotary action helping out in all adjustments; it is

* An example of "set-ups" mentioned on p. 38. [Eds.]

always on tap. One needs to see to it that there is an alert action, a technique for a repeated action at the elbow, which is always producing movement of the hand.

The wrist joint must furnish the ball bearings which allow this smooth freedom of hand movement. But that can only happen if the hand is not involved with positive actions of its own initiative, but, instead, acts as a supplement to the activity in the two large levers.

If the technique of the hand is one of supplementing the activity in the upper arm and forearm, what about the fingers? The fingers contact the key, and their primary function is to stand up under the power which is delivered by the other levers. They vitalize when the power comes along and, by that vitalization, share the action of striking the key, but they do not *initiate* this action.

Then why the Czerny and Hanon exercises? It is precisely to counteract the damage done by trying to develop the fingers in hitting power that this analysis of the mechanism which makes the Etudes fluent is being made. All the hours of Czerny and Hanon have rarely resulted in a masterful playing of the Etudes. They often have done quite the reverse. If the Etudes are played with mastery it is because the rest of the mechanism does the work — not the fingers.*

The fingers space for the power of the big levers to be delivered to a chord. *The manner in which they space is very important.* It must not be a reaching with the tip of the finger. It must be a spacing which takes place in the palm, and the fingers extend that palm action. Here again is a situation where words are apt to fail utterly in conveying the desired action, because fingers have the habit of reaching for key position. They have been trained to do just that. One of the results of this reaching with

* One might even go further and say that when a masterful playing is achieved by a gifted student who practiced Czerny and Hanon, etc., this mastery was achieved in spite of his practicing these exercises and not because of it. [Eds.]

the fingers will be a shutting off of the power of the big levers at the wrist. The wrist is much less free when fingers are reaching for position.

For a sensation of achieving a control for chord formation in the palm, close the fingers lightly into a fist (no sense of gripping). Then, spread the distance across the row of hand knuckles and the palm segment of the thumb. The spread between knuckles will be a tiny amount, but the palm segment of the thumb can spread out considerably, like a fan opening. (This spreading varies greatly with different hands. Some have a visible amount of play between knuckles, and some have practically none. The hands with a tight ligamentous attachment are the hands which have difficulty with large chords even when the hand is large.) When the spread across the knuckles and with the palm segment of the thumb has been made and well sensed, then open the fingers and thumb to full length while the control of their spacing remains in the palm. It is only when this kind of palm-spacing takes place for chords and octaves that the wrist can easily remain flexible and free. Without a wrist which is always ready to let the power back of it through into the hand and fingers there will never be a superlative technical equipment.

In all the statements made it is taken for granted that the aim in any coordination is to tap the full resources of the performer for grace and beauty in interpretation as well as for brilliance with speed.

As we proceed to the analysis of each Etude, there will, of necessity, be endless repetition. If out of that repetition there emerges the realization that, in fact, there are not various kinds of techniques but only the same fundamental actions in various proportions, then perhaps the repetition can be borne.

Each Etude brings into relief a special balance in activity. One can say, "Here are the ingredients. For this or that Etude add a bit more of this or that action."

In these Etudes there is a completely fascinating handling of the various problems of a skilled coordination. There is no other set of Etudes which so comprehensively presents every necessary aspect of virtuosity, always combined with musical beauty. They are expert, beyond belief, in dealing with every need. They hit the nail on the head every time, and at the same time they are musically delightful. They are real Etudes — they give no respite from the problem of the moment. There is no breathing space — no break in the pattern — so that muscles can be rested and ready for a fresh spurt of energy. That is why they are so difficult.

There must be a perfect balance in the controls for distance and power, or these Etudes will continue to be difficult.

Unless teachers are sufficiently expert in suggesting a coordination without interfering with nature's plan by stressing a specific kind of movement, the chances are that teaching will not further the coordination needed to play the Etudes.

The ingredients to be used are:

I. AN ACCURATE AURAL IMAGE

II. A BASIC RHYTHM AND A RHYTHM OF METER

III. A COMPLETELY COORDINATED BODY AND ARM FOR THE CONTROL OF DISTANCE — HORIZONTAL, VERTICAL, AND IN-AND-OUT

IV. A COMPLETELY COORDINATED BODY AND ARM FOR THE USE OF POWER

I. AURAL IMAGE

There can be no expert movement unless the movement is made to produce a specific tone. Only the ear can dictate that specific tone.

Before work for the coordination of learning a piece starts, one should hear what is to be played.

If the printed page does not mean specific tones to you, and it doesn't unless pitch perception is very keen, learn the sound of the tones by playing each tone with a full-arm stroke.* Have the upper arm completely responsible for the tone. Don't pretend to the coordination which will be used for playing later. Just sound the tones with a full-arm stroke until the ear has the image of the printed page.

There will be no speed with this mechanism, but there can and should be continuity in action because of the circular joint at the shoulder through which the upper arm is working.

Faulty first impressions are to be avoided, if possible, because first impressions have a way of lasting. With the full-arm stroke playing each tone, there is less damage done to the desired final coordination in a first reading, because continuity in action is possible with the upper arm in control of tone.

II. RHYTHM

The rhythm of note values — meter — is a part of the larger rhythm of form. This rhythm of meter is taken care of in the process of articulating details.

But it is the basic rhythm of form — of the musical idea as a unit — which is the educator, the interpreter, the coordinator, and the creator of beauty in a performance. This rhythm must be installed before any performance can ripen into its fullest beauty. With this basic rhythm in command, fresh impressions of the meaning of the music never cease to appear.

"We learn by doing," John Dewey has taught us, and certainly in making music the kind of doing can either open new avenues of learning constantly or it can hamper the growth in awareness of the subtleties which create exquisite phrase modeling.

Upper arm and torso create and implement the basic rhythm. The upper arm makes articulate the mood of the torso (a) as it gauges all distance (horizontal, vertical, and in-and-out), (b) as it uses its power for initiating tone production, (c) as it acts as fulcrum for forearm. The

* See Glossary.

torso does its creating in two ways: (a) by responding to the mood of the music, (b) by acting as a fulcrum for the playing mechanism.

III. DISTANCE

Horizontal, Vertical and In-and-Out

1. Horizontal distance is the length of the keyboard — treble to bass.
2. Vertical distance is the distance of key depression (key-drop).
3. In-and-out distance is created by (a) the difference in the distance of the black and white keys from the body, (b) the difference in length and operational point between the thumb and the fingers.

Torso

Horizontal distance: The torso leans right or left to make readily available the use of arms in treble or bass. Other movements, which one sees, are made in response to the emotional reaction to the music, not really to facilitate distance.

Upper Arm

Horizontal, vertical, and in-and-out distance: The upper arm, by turnings of the humerus, *gauges* the action for *all* distance and, in so doing, there can be a coordination of the whole arm for sharing distance — a prime necessity for achieving virtuosity in handling distance.

Forearm

The forearm covers horizontal and vertical distance by flexion and extension. Also, by the *twisting* and *untwisting* of its rotary action, the forearm moves the hand along the keyboard in somewhat the same way a measuring worm makes progress; it takes key-drop with the same movements.

Forearm and Hand

In-and-out distance: Forearm and hand provide excellent coverage. A *high wrist* means flexion with both forearm and hand, and this combined action brings the hand closer to the torso. A *low wrist* means extension with both forearm and hand, which puts the hand farther away from the torso. The *forearm*, not the hand, is the instigator of these actions.

Hand

Horizontal distance: The lateral movement of the hand is not large, but it is important in passage work.

Vertical distance is easily covered by flexion and extension of the hand.

In-and-out distance: Flexion and extension of the hand combine with flexion and extension of the forearm.

Fingers

The fingers help to cover *horizontal distance* by a spread which is controlled at the hand knuckle. They help in taking *vertical distance* by an easy flexion and extension at the hand knuckle. Flexion and extension at all three joints help in covering in-and-out distance.

Thumb

The thumb participates in covering *horizontal distance* by abduction and adduction.

With abduction and adduction there can be enough rotation to take *vertical distance* (key-drop).

Unless all control of the thumb is initiated with the segment which is a part of the palm — at the wrist joint — there may be a considerable loss in the span of the hand, and chords and octaves may be needlessly difficult.

IV. POWER

All power for tone production is applied through a vertical key action with a down stroke. Any lever with a vertical action can apply power with that action. *But*, if the power of a vertical action is unrelated to a continuous action toward a destination, then we have a notewise procedure — a separate initiation of power for each tone — and a notewise procedure is the very antithesis of a basic rhythm. Separate initiations of power allow only a rhythm of meter — note values — which is no rhythm at all for grace and subtle phrase moulding. A basic rhythm, a physical action which is the counterpart of the musical idea as a whole, is the all-important movement for grace and subtlety in phrase moulding. Continuity toward a destination implies the completion of an idea. The musical idea is registered by the ear as a meaningful statement, and this statement has a beginning and an end — a destination. In performance the procedure to the completion of the statement is made vivid and realistic by a physical movement which is the counterpart of the musical idea, a movement which has continuity from the beginning to the end of the musical idea — a phrasewise rhythm.

The glissando is the simplest and most direct manipulation at the keyboard for going straight to the destination; the ripped chord is the next in simplicity. In both illustrations there is speed in procedure, and this speed emphasizes the one fundamental action which goes from beginning to end, taking in a group of tones on the way. In both illustrations it was the upper arm which produced the fundamental action. In both illustrations the power of this upper arm operated at the bottom of the key-drop (key bed). In both illustrations the sensation was of vigorous action toward a goal — not of stopping and sticking against key bed.

Maintaining these simple, fundamental relationships is the key to the solution of the technical problems found in the Chopin Etudes.

To be aware of the activity which forms new habits it is necessary to use a slow tempo, and with a slow tempo we are immediately confronted with the wholly undesirable tendency to stop (stand still) between tones and to use pressure against the key bed after tone has been produced. These two faulty actions are the exact opposite of the desired activity for both grace and speed in playing. Therefore be certain that, no matter how slow the tempo, the activity between tones (the going forward to the goal) remains the commanding activity, and the action of articulating tones must not take precedence over it.

Try slowing down the ripped chord (first five tones of the C major scale) and see just how difficult it is to keep as strong a sense, as was evident with speed, of one action controlling the going forward. See how almost impossible it is to make the fingers wait upon the arrival of the fundamental power of the upper arm for part of the tone production. The fact that there is time between tones gives the ear a chance to listen to separate tones with greater intensity, and the physical response to that aural intensity is emphasis on the vertical action related to producing that pitch. Hearing the five tones as a unit tends to disappear as the fundamental continuous action of the upper arm for going forward disappears.

When you succeed in playing these five tones in a slow tempo inside the progress of the power of the upper arm, even when the tones are staccato, then a basic relationship of leverage for the use of power has been established which will facilitate the playing of the Etudes.

The Etudes which help in emphasizing the use of the two large levers (upper arm and forearm) will be taken first. That does not mean that they are the easiest but, simply, that their technical difficulties graphically illustrate the use of the mechanism which is basic for all of the Etudes.

Etude, Op. 10, No. 7

When one can play Op. 10, No. 7 at top speed without a cramp in the forearm the coordination *has* to be right; the bulk of the work *has* to be done with the upper arm and forearm, and this same coordination functions in every one of the Etudes.

There is a simple principle in operation in the most complicated passages: *Let the powerful levers do the work.*

Op. 10, No. 7 is perfect for learning this principle. It is the only one of the Etudes which never varies in the number of articulations used by one action of the large levers: One movement of the upper arm produces one articulation; one movement of the forearm produces one articulation.* Train these large levers to initiate the controls of distance and power, and technical difficulties are diminished a hundredfold.

The fact that a complicated anatomy operates this mechanism need not concern us. We can trust nature to use the mechanism with the utmost of skill if we do not build up barriers by establishing faulty habits which prevent the principle from working.

These two powerful levers are farthest away from the keyboard. They cannot be effective in controlling distance and power unless the hand is sufficiently passive † and delicately balanced so that every action by the powerful levers gets through the wrist joint. And, in turn, the fingers are passive, except for maintaining the span of the thirds and the sixths, and furnishing the bones against which the power back of them is delivered. Getting the feel of the action of the two large levers is the all-important first step, before actual playing takes place.

Work on the premise that the two large levers do all the work. They really do most of it, and believing that they do all of it, plus having a wrist that is always barely-once-removed from being relaxed, gives nature the helm in coordinating the actions of hand and fingers.

Use the upper arm (a pull) for the thirds. Use the forearm (extension, down-action) for the sixths. To stimulate a vivid sensing of these two actions, place the hand flat on the surface of the keys (just as you would rest it lightly on a table, palm down and flat). Then use a quick, vigorous pull with the upper arm, flexing the forearm as a complement of this pull. Let anything happen that will at the keyboard — just don't pay attention to the hand or fingers. But, do pay attention to a quick, vigorous, short

* See Foreword, pp. 11–12.

† By "passive" the author does not mean a flabby hand. See p. 63 for detailed description. [Eds.]

pull of the upper arm which automatically uses a flexion
of forearm as a part of its action.

Then use a quick extension of the forearm, allowing
the end of the forearm (the base of the palm) to put the
keys down. This quick extension of forearm will do two
things: It will throw the hand out and up, and it will raise
the tip of the elbow slightly (the muscles governing action
of the forearm lie in the upper arm, and their vigorous
action always moves the upper arm slightly). Note that
a continuous holding activity in the upper arm must coordinate all the diverse actions.

If the hand refuses to stay out of these actions (because
it has been trained to feel the keyboard) practice these
two vigorous actions at a table until there is a definite
awareness that the two large levers are in full command
of all the movements taking place. Then return to the
keyboard and duplicate the passive activity of the hand.
Let the hand splash around at the will of the upper arm
and forearm. Learn this relationship well — very, very
well. The playing mechanism will never achieve virtuosity
without it (the kind of virtuosity the jazz people have
without an eight-hour-a-day workout). The step from the
hand being passive (out of the picture) to having it furnish the bones for articulation should be simple. But
nothing is really simple if there are established habits
which go counter to a desired relationship. It may take
an astonishing amount of patient persistence and care to
keep the same free wrist and lack of initiation of action
by the hand and fingers when the ear dictates that the
third and sixth are to be sounded (repeating the same
third and sixth — we are still not attempting an extended
pattern).

Actually, it is not possible to will a change in relationships of leverage and have it stick in a fast tempo. One can
achieve it in a very slow, controlled tempo if there is real
understanding and care; but the moment the tempo is
increased beyond a detailed control, old habits will take
over. (In my experience, exceptions to this rule have been

very rare.) There is no way of achieving a dependable control except through constantly seeking new ways of sensing this new relationship of having the large levers take over.

Do not avoid the simple first steps. Do not take it for granted that now you have learned the new coordination. The old habits will persist and thwart you if you do, and one tends to take too much for granted too soon. This fundamental relationship of large levers to hand and fingers is the basis of all virtuosity. We need it — have to have it for Op. 10, No. 7 — and for every Etude which follows. So, clarify the sensation of this relationship with great care. Only as this relationship of the two large levers (upper arm and forearm) initiating the controls for articulation becomes a reality can the Etude be played.

The basic rhythm becomes the greatest assistance in establishing this relationship. Think of the juggler as we start the analysis for playing the Etude: Doing one thing never interferes with the continuity of the complete routine. Every separate act is inside the rhythm of the over-all pattern. So it is with playing a phrase: *Each articulation of tone must be inside the basic rhythm* (the "routine" of the juggler) which is the action that forms the phrase as a whole, or the phrase ceases to be an integrated whole. The latter happens when the hand or fingers cease to wait for the upper arm to initiate the going forward.

There is an order in the procedure, the coordination, which produces a smooth, whole phrase (just as there is order with the whole routine of the juggler), and it is imperative that we become aware of the relationship in that order so that it can work for us and help to smooth out all the difficulties. First, we have the aural image. Second, we react emotionally to the sound of the imaged music. Third, we produce the imaged tones.

The emotional reaction to the music should produce the basic rhythm, *but unfortunately an emotional reaction does not insure a basic rhythm.* Two reactions are possible:

one, to the phrase as a whole — a meaningful, musical statement (a basic rhythm); two, a reaction to the production of single tones, which destroys a meaningful musical statement — a rhythm of meter or note values.

These two kinds of emotional reaction can classify all performances: the performances which make music — allow it to flow, and the performances which distort the music with far too many climaxes and the stressing of too many single tones. One performer plays with a basic rhythm — a rhythm of form; the other performer stresses the rhythm of meter — single tones.

Thus, it becomes of paramount importance that we understand and insure the use of the rhythm of form at the beginning of studying a composition. A performance of these Etudes which has both virtuosity and grace can not be achieved without this rhythm.

There is nothing mysterious about this rhythm. It is as simple as skating or dancing and is just like them, except that we are limited to sitting on a chair instead of moving about. In skating and dancing it is the swaying, balanced follow-through of the body — the gliding along from one highlight to another — which enhances the feeling of the music.

Exactly the same follow-through can take place in the torso when we are sitting; and there we have the emotional response to the music with a rhythm which fits the mood and form of the music.

Just use the torso for feeling the musical mood. It is as simple as that.

There is no one way of using the torso. Simply allow it the freedom to feel and respond with action to the music. The important thing is to respond emotionally. One needs only to observe the artists who create great beauty to become convinced that there is a tremendous response in their whole being to the music which possesses them.

If music, beautifully phrased, pours forth with this emotional response in their bodies, rest assured that this emotional response is an important part of their playing. If it is important for them it is assuredly important for us to learn to be free in expressing emotion with our bodies. It is *the essential physical activity* in response to the aural image if we are to create beauty. Therefore, let us take up directly the study of rhythm.

A primary tool for achieving a basic rhythm is outlining a composition. This means playing the highlights and omitting details (some of the notes of the music). In leaving out details remember that the sole purpose is to emphasize the structural outline of the music. If this outlining is done in a cut-and-dried fashion, without the emotional response to the music, it is of *no value*. It is only when the outlining intensifies the grace of going forward with a lilting step, as it were, that it illuminates, quickens, and frees the emotional rhythm in the torso.

No one should say, "The outline must be just this way and no other." There is always the possibility of choices. Here are several possibilities of outlining the first bar of Op. 10, No. 7:

1 B

*

* Staccato marks are a reminder that practicing the outline of a new piece is preferably done *staccato*, because a sense of buoyancy, rather than stodginess, is more easily achieved.

1 C

1 D

1 E

Remember the reason for outlining is to enhance the basic rhythm in the torso. Make a swinging continuity the one imperative achievement — *not accuracy in key hitting.* The aural image should be established and *accurate* before the outlining begins.* Once started with the outlining, let it dance — accuracy or no accuracy — until the rhythm possesses you, and you feel a compelling desire to move with the music.

Move how? Twist, turn, sway, bounce — just anything you feel like doing, using the resistance of the ischial bones against the chair seat as you would use your feet against the floor if you were standing. Or, there can be an emotional holding in the torso which, in some cases, shows very little overt activity, but which, nonetheless, furnishes the same intensity in the continuity of progression.

But, above all, *be active.* Learn to know you have a torso when playing. Set it free and *exult* in its freedom if you want to play like Rachmaninoff. You will play with much less beauty and excitement, if you think of how you look instead of feeling the thrill of action.

The ears cannot turn the trick alone — a rhythm must help them out, and a real rhythm means physical activity.

Being successful with outlining will mean an emotional reaction to this Etude's gay little dance which creates an aliveness in activity from chair seat to keyboard — a unified activity of body and arms. Don't stop outlining until this emotional reaction commands the playing. If the playing is only a perfunctory achievement the outlining has not been put to full use.

If the pianist has no relation between the arms and a rhythm in the body during performance, then the emotional reaction will be expressed with the hitting process — striking the key — and this is the situation which em-

---

* See Foreword. At a later stage A. W. felt that an accurate aural image of details should be worked for after a dance-like basic rhythm has been established. For further discussion see section on "splashing." [Eds.]

phasizes details at the expense of the feeling of the music as a whole.

The bass is a powerful ally of the rhythm of form. Give it concentrated attention. Note that if the first beats of the first two measures set the pace, a long swinging stride takes hold of the music. Keep this stride by being increasingly aware of the bass.*

It is very easy for the ear to get involved with the melody of the soprano (we always speak of "right hand" — never right arm, which it certainly should be; this is a pertinent part of our hand consciousness instead of arm consciousness). The detailed discussion will emphasize the soprano part because the technical difficulty lies there, but caution must be maintained to keep the pulsing rhythm in the bass a vital, *emotional* part of the playing. Installing a basic rhythm imposes the problem of utilizing both the process of listening and a physical response of the rhythm of form.

Good jazz players all keep this balance between ear and the physical activity. We can learn much from them. It is this balance which helps to give them their great facility.

Learning a new piece tends to make the pianist listen notewise. The better the ear, the more it listens for each individual sound. But the music was written phrasewise at all stages; from the initial studying to the final polished performance a balance between ear and a basic rhythm must be kept for a superlative interpretation.

Rhythm for the performer is expressed through physical activity — an activity which must be emotionally vital to him. "Make your own dynamite," said Myra Hess, after listening to a gifted young pianist who failed to express the emotional intensity of the music. We are too much aware of the production of details and too little aware of the production of this emotional rhythmic intensity.

* One of the tools most frequently used by the author to make the bass important was to have the student play the bass with both hands one or two octaves apart — depending on the musical texture. [Eds.]

Refer to page 50, where we dealt with the two large levers for delivering power for tone. Now, in dealing with a segment of the outline (pp. 54–55) there is the all-important demand for the continuity in action which produces the musical idea rather than the individual tones. (Exs. 1–1ᴇ.) The slow-motion picture of a polo pony in action is an excellent illustration for this combination. When the film is slowed down, the continuity in action between applications of power against the ground becomes much more evident than the actual points of contact. We see with such vividness the projection of the body from one contact with the ground to the next.

It may not be easy to isolate the awareness of the movement of the upper arm when multiple actions are involved, but it is precisely this smooth continuity in progression with the upper arm (like the slowed-down picture of the polo pony) that is the action which initiates and maintains control when playing is at its very best.

Smooth, continuous progression with the actions for the control of distance, and the initiation of power for tone in the upper arm form the basis for subtle handling of the multiple actions of the whole arm.

Expert timing is always the result of subdividing a large time unit created by the movement of the large lever from start to destination, rather than the addition of several small time units one to the other.

Ex. 2

When *a* to *g* has become an established time unit through the smooth continuity of the upper arm, then we

* In Examples 2–2f the first half of measure 1 is used instead of a complete phrase. This is done only for convenience in presenting several examples. When familiarity with this procedure is established, extend the musical unit to at least two bars.

shall play the details in between *b, c, d, e, f* with accuracy, better spacing, and greater facility.

Using a full-arm stroke* (which means complete control of distance and power with the upper arm while the rest of the arm simply extends that control — as a conductor's baton extends his arm) set up a smooth, rhythmic playing of *a* and *g* thirds with complete regularity.

Attend to the evenness of progression between the thirds. It must be like the slow-motion picture of the polo pony — no sticking, no stopping, but complete evenness in the physical action of arriving and departing between the playing of the thirds.

Then heed well: Without disturbing this smooth progression and regularity, tuck in third *e* and then *c*. Do not let the tucking-in process stop the smooth swing back to *a*. Do not tuck in *c* and *e* on every swing from *a* to *g*. Keep the strong sensation of the larger unit of time and the smooth action producing it, by using only the swing from *a* to *g* at least as often as the tucking-in process is used.

* See Glossary.

Review once more page 50 and, time and again, go through the actions which establish the correct relationship between the two large levers and the hand.

Now that we are articulating details of a pattern all action becomes complex, but for the present ignore that fact. Nature is far smarter than we are: If we attend to simplicity in action by the large levers nature will take care of the rest.

First, play from *a* to *g* to allow a definite feeling of destination to be achieved. When *c* and *e* are safely tucked in without disturbing the continuity of action from *a* to *g*, let *f* be tucked in with a forearm extension (page 60, Ex. 2D). Be certain that the forearm, not the hand nor

2 D

a   c   e f   g

the fingers, supplements the upper-arm power for playing the sixth and also takes the key-drop. Repeatedly return to the basic progressions by leaving out the complications. Practice the relationship of large levers to the hand (page 50). Then, with the same routine of tucking in, add *d* and finally *b*.

2 E

a   c   d   e   f   g

2 F

a   b   c   d   e f   g

It is important to observe the sequence of the tucking-in process. When the destination is strongly felt, there will be less chance for its interruption if the last third and the last sixth etc. are tucked in first. The larger action has then been given its chance to get under way. There is far greater chance of the large action being interrupted if one begins tucking in at the inception of the large movement. The fact that the ear must control the playing makes this sequence of outline that much more important. If the ear is headed for *g* it will take *e* more easily on the way than it will take *c*. The same thing, of course, holds with the sixths. Once again: *It is practicing the most basic controls first and most often that produces the fastest results in the finished product.* Include the details too often and too soon and no new coordination will get established which will accept the details in their rightful relation to the whole.

Return frequently to the basic, rhythmic outline and feel afresh the dance-like lilt of the music; be increasingly aware of the importance of the left hand (arm) in implementing the dance. Enjoy the outline and, every now and then, include the details.

The study of the complete Etude should follow the sequence used in the small excerpt: Have a strong feeling for the dance-like outline and the sense of going forward before all the notes are tucked in. Periodically omit the details to be sure that the outlining is still the important sensation.

It is always the basic structure of the music which needs the most cultivation. When it is sturdy and authoritative the details can be added without damage to the strong rhythmic force which is the reaction to the musical statement as a whole. This relationship of simplicity to complexity (large form to details) is an absolute necessity both for musical grace and for a balanced coordination.

The only change in the musical pattern comes at the fourth measure from the end. There should be no change in the relationship of large levers to the hand, except that now the sixth is played with the upper-arm pull and the single tone with the extension of the forearm.

Even though the upper arm and the forearm do a large percentage of all the work, there has to be a vitalization at wrist and finger joints at the split second when power for tone is delivered. This activity of the hand and fingers permits the upper arm and forearm to function effectively so that a feeling of boniness and general deftness pervades the performance.

Two operations are always taking place: the finding of the key, and the delivery of power for tone. There is bound to be consistent difficulty with the Etudes unless the pianist differentiates between the two operations. (Because of the traditional training given to the fingers and hand, it is assumed that there are faulty habits to be dealt with. There never need be any awareness of the physical activity in playing if there are no difficulties. The ears and rhythm can function perfectly if no faulty habits block their functioning.) Finding the key — having a fluent technique for covering distance — demands a relationship in which a tiny action at the center of the radius of activity (the shoulder joint) will produce a wide skip, if necessary, at the hand. It is like the crack of a whip: A tiny action at the handle produces a wide flourish at the tip. To make this action efficient every joint between the shoulder and fingers must be so delicately active that the lever it controls can be very easily jarred into movement. It is in this relationship to the coverage of distance at the keyboard that a free wrist is of inestimable value, actually a necessity. There is not apt to be a blockage to a quick flip from the shoulder at the elbow or with rotary; but, if the hand has been trained for finding position and producing independent power there is sure to be insufficient freedom at the wrist joint for letting the hand be propelled by a larger lever.

Until the wrist joint carries the hand in such a delicate balance that there is no resistance to a shake from the upper arm, there will be no superlative technique for covering the distance of the keyboard.

Doubtless this relationship of freedom at all joints will

be more easily sensed away from the keyboard, when the ear is not dictating pitch, and former reactions to that dictation are not operating.

Shake the hand free until the wrist offers no resistance to its movement in any direction. Complete relaxation is not the idea, because in actual playing this would be an obstacle to speed. Either close the hand lightly or carry some small, light object in the hand so that there is a controlled activity in the hand while the wrist lets go. Then go back to the keyboard and see if the hand can maintain an easy chord formation as it is thrown for a large skip. The wrist must be just as free in a diatonic passage, but exaggeration in distance helps to make the play at wrist more evident.

When this free play at all joints has been sensed, and the key has been located, then the operation for delivering power for tone takes place. The muscles furnish the power, but the bony structure furnishes the resistive element which makes that power effective.

For efficiency in the use of power the large muscles must take the major portion of the action for producing tone — never the small muscles of the hand and fingers. This involves the element of timing without which perfection and top-notch performance are never attained, whether in music or in sports. The upper arm initiates the energy, and instantly the arm becomes one unified bone from shoulder to finger tip, as power is delivered through every joint.

This operation, of necessity, works from shoulder to finger tip — center to periphery. A hand which has been trained for independent action will almost certainly block this natural coordination from center to periphery. The hand is at the keyboard. If it acts independently then its action arrives ahead of any arm power.

Strain and inefficiency always result if the small muscles governing the hand and fingers are overworked, as they almost always will be when they are trained to reach for the key and to produce independent power for tone.

When the action of small muscles is a component part of the total mechanism, then distance is no longer a hazard, and brilliance can be achieved with speed.*

Certainly it is imagery to say that neither the hand nor fingers produce any power for tone, that the function is simply to furnish their bones for the large muscles to play against. But, it is the kind of imagery which will produce results.

The hand and fingers must carry the form of the thirds and sixths constantly. The thirds do not let go while the sixths are played nor do the sixths relax while the thirds are played. This chord formation is a control in the palm — not ever at the tip of the fingers. Imagine the skeleton of the hand and consciously move only the bones in the palm. The fingers will move at the hand knuckle as an extension of the palm bones.

There are two places in the Etude which will illustrate the difference in ease with the right control of distance and power as opposed to a faulty control: bars 24–25 and 48–51. These places will remain difficult so long as the fingers make the slightest effort to reach for position or to produce tone. Give over the control of placement (lateral distance) to the upper arm and make the hand do nothing but furnish the bones for standing under power, and instantly these measures lose their difficulty. Think of the basic rhythm while working to have the upper arm assume control of placement. Separate the succeeding articulations by a skip of an octave. (Ex. 3.) It will be much easier

Ex. 3

* The author was aware that some pianists of major talent, in spite of such training, manage to achieve the use of a basic rhythm without consciously working for it. It is only right to stress that even the possession of such an overwhelming talent does not always prevent a student from being either ruined or severely handicapped by the faulty teaching she refers to. [Eds.]

to become aware of the activity in the upper arm when the distance is exaggerated.

This Etude can and should be played without any ache in the forearm. So long as there is a pain in the forearm it definitely means that the fingers are working more than they should. An excellent aid in getting rid of this habit of reaching for position with the fingers is to increase the awareness of the sensation of the arm as one bone.

With every freshly acquired sensation of increased initiation of power in the upper arm there is a strong tendency among students to think, "Now I have it." Everything will seem easier the moment a block is removed, because of an increased response in the upper arm to the aural image. But perfection is always a matter of refining and refining the sensation of the arm as a unit — one continuous bone at the very moment tone is produced.

Become increasingly aware of this bony structure. It is a valuable help in getting rid of reaching with fingers, and that reaching habit is eradicated very slowly. Fingers only give up when the upper arm produces the initial response to the aural image. The forearm is always involved with the action of the upper arm (review page 50 — "placing the hand"). This Etude produces only one articulation with each miniature pull of the upper arm while the forearm *flexes* and one articulation while the forearm *extends;* the result of the forearm action is great speed. All such speed in repeating an action involves a large expenditure of energy and produces a feeling of tension. The tension is caused by the constant fast contraction of the muscles. In this situation it is very easy to become conscious of the forearm action, to the exclusion of being aware of the easier action of the upper arm. The upper-arm action is never a simple, repeated action like the action of a hinge joint. More muscles are involved at the circular shoulder joint, and more than one control is operating at the same time — one of its tremendous assets.

So, whenever the upper-arm action is ignored and ceases to be consistently active for its multiple controls, an extra burden is placed on activity elsewhere. The result of this imbalance in activity is sufficient cause for failure in achievement in playing this Etude with virtuosity.*

Thus, constantly refer to the basic rhythm — refresh the sensation of the dancing outline. Put the upper arm through its controls for proceeding toward a destination with the smooth action that is like the slow-motion picture of the polo pony. Become aware of the control of level with the upper arm, as in the glissando and the ripped chord, so that its control of finding the key involves a sliding into and on to the next key-drop. Only a basic rhythm, with control of placement in the upper arm plus energy for tone production both as it articulates tone and gauges the level at which tone is produced, can produce a balanced use of energy. Without a perfect balance in the use of energy, which means all possible conservation of energy, no pianist will play this Etude with virtuosity and beauty.

Etude, Op. 25, No. 10

This Etude demands the same balance in activity between the operation of the upper arm and the repeated action of the forearm as Op. 10, No. 7. But now, the need to maintain an octave span adds to the chances for strain in the hand. Another difference is that frequently there are multiple articulations of tone to one initiation of power by the upper arm.

This Etude is marked legato in all editions. Legato playing, as conventionally taught, requires that one hold

* Later on this analysis became still further refined: A. W. stated that the activity of a pull operates in such a way that even the "miniature pulls" are absorbed inside an activity of a continuous pull. For instance, she demonstrated that even when the upper arm moves forward a pull can operate continuously because of the extraordinarily complex interaction of muscles working through the shoulder joint. [Eds.]

a key down until the next one is played. Since the piano tone starts to diminish the moment the key is struck, holding down the key is not the action which in a fast tempo produces a feeling of legato. The ear hears a phrase as legato when the dynamics (volume of tone at its inception) of the successive tones of that phrase form a smooth curve of intensities which leads the ear forward to a completed statement.*

Even with a complete key connection for legato, if the dynamics have no relation to progression in the musical statement the ear will still hear the phrase as non-legato. Test this out. Now, there is nothing that hampers speed more than the habit of holding the key down after tone is produced. The basis for all speed is the shortest possible application of power for tone.

But the "shortest possible application of power" does not involve a complementary up-action, so often taught as the basis of staccato playing. It simply means the cessation of the use of power. The key will come up if it is not held down. The disconnection of the power, when speed is involved, will take place at the first finger joint (hand-knuckle joint) or at the wrist or at both these joints, while the two large levers are involved with the finding of the key and the production of power for the succeeding tone.

A faulty use of legato or staccato will never result in fast, brilliant octaves. This Etude is always played (when it is played brilliantly) as nearly staccato as possible. Great speed prevents a time unit between tones which allows the ear to hear disconnection.

---

* In this connection it is of interest to quote from the preface to Book I of *The Well Tempered Clavier*, edited by D. F. Tovey and fingered by Harold Samuel. On page xiii (recommending the cultivation of a "legato" while using the fifth finger only): ". . . . . . and will learn that pianoforte polyphony requires . . . . . . a balance of tone which cannot be attained when the hand is preoccupied with squirming in order to avoid infinitesimal discontinuities and overlaps which the ear does not notice at all. On the pianoforte a breach of *legato* is

When a slow tempo is used in the learning process, always see to it that the same "shortest possible application of power" is being practiced; this is imperative for ultimate speed. Slow practice is responsible for a multitude of habits which are detrimental for achieving speed unless the "shortest possible application of power" for tone is used.

The following is very important to remember: The octave span can be easy or it can produce strain, depending on the manner in which it is held. Two factors are involved: (1) The action for the span must utilize the right muscles. (2) The holding of the span must use the absolute minimum of muscular effort necessary to maintain the spread. The right muscles are the ones which open the palm; the wrong muscles are those which produce a sensation of reaching at the tip of the fingers.

For achieving a definite sensation of opening the palm without bringing the wrong muscles into play, close the hand into a very, very lightly held fist and then spread the knuckles at the base of the fingers. At the same time, with the thumb still flexed as in fist formation, abduct the palm segment of the thumb. Now there will be a spread in the palm from the little finger knuckle to the first knuckle of the thumb (the knuckle next to the wrist joint). Repeat the action until there is an easily governed spreading of the palm from the little finger knuckle to the first thumb knuckle. Then extend the fingers and thumb until they fit an octave, holding the spread with all delicacy — as though thistle down were inside the fist.

This palm activity must become a natural, habitual response to the need for an octave before the fingers will give up all activity of reaching; and until the fingers do

---

not so often a gap as a bump in the tone: and it is sometimes produced at its worst by the very means taken to avoid gaps." (From J. S. Bach, *Forty-eight Preludes and Fugues.* Copyright 1924 by the Associated Board of the R.A.M. and the R.C.M. Renewed 1951 by the Associated Board of the Royal Schools of Music. Printed by permission of the American agents—Mills Music, Inc.)

give up, there will be no easy, free wrist which is a necessity for fluent octaves. Remember, the wrist must allow
the hand to be propelled into position with the same relationship to the initial gauging of distance by the upper
arm and flexion of the forearm as was described on page
50.

Frequently there are tones inside the octave span to
be played. They must be spaced with the same lack of
reaching with the tip of the finger as the octave. This
spacing, if the hand is small or has a tight ligamentous
attachment at the knuckles, may be assisted by a slight
change in the position of the hand. There can be an adjustment at shoulder, elbow, and wrist to facilitate the
taking of the chord, but there cannot be a reaching with
the finger tip without damage to facility.

These middle tones are written as half-notes and
quarter-notes as though they should be held. Actually
what is desired is that these middle tones should be important in sound. It will be the manner of using dynamics
which will make these tones important — not the length
of time they are held. Trying to hold these middle tones
(keeping the keys down) complicates the playing without
producing any results tangible to the ear. The fact is,
these middle tones are not held in a virtuoso performance
any more than the octaves are played legato. The relationship of the activity of the upper arm to multiple
articulations — one continuous action by the first big
lever absorbing the action of the other levers — is far
too complicated in the balance of activity to be factually
set forth; but nature plus imagery will turn the trick
if given a chance. Cling to the simple concept of having
the large lever do the work and repeatedly play glis-
sandos and ripped chords to get a vivid awareness of the
activity of the upper arm. One pull from the shoulder
produces all of the tones without any consciousness of the
other actions involved in these simple tone patterns.

One *continuous* activity at the shoulder must be a
valuable initial force for producing several octaves. The

controls operating with this continuous activity of the upper arm are:

I. *Finding the key* (as in the glissando and ripped chord): Use wide skips — the entire length of the keyboard — with no thought except to observe the action of the upper arm. By a turning of the humerus, the elbow will describe an arc B, and the hand will describe a larger arc A. When there is no large skip but, instead, only the distance between consecutive keys, there should be no change in the relation of controls; a miniature turn of the humerus is still the controlling factor for the movement into position.

II. *Gauging, maintaining a sense of the level where tone is produced* (as in the glissando and ripped chord): In using a close position on the keyboard when speed is called for, the finding of the key is achieved while a consistent level is maintained. Now the arcs become smaller and smaller until the elbow seems to be moving horizontally. Exaggeration of the control of the upper arm will assist in observing the turns of the humerus: Imagine the upper arm as a very large pencil whose point is the elbow. Use a table top and place the elbow point in actual contact with the surface as the arcs are drawn. Then, have the finger tips also contact the surface.

It will be perfectly obvious that these table-top arcs lack the complications involved in using the keyboard: (a) The elbow point does not touch the keyboard. (b) There is a constant adjustment to in-and-out distance at shoulder, elbow, and wrist joint. Nevertheless, the table-top arcs can vivify the relationship in controls. First, and of extreme importance, for virtuosity with octaves it is the elbow (and therefore the upper arm) which is primarily keeping contact with the table top and has the feeling of staying down. The forearm and hand are not bearing down but, instead, are very light in their feeling and just moved about by the upper arm.

Search relentlessly for any exaggeration or imagery which produces this sensation in relationship between the first big lever and the rest of the arm. Also, be willing to spend time to become extremely conscious of the many degrees of refinement which are possible in the balance of activity in the arm within the relationship of the first lever retaining over-all control, while the rest of the arm (forearm, hand, etc.) stays alert, supple, and very light. (It is this relationship which has given rise to the term "a hanging elbow" but this term does not suggest the necessary activity.)

Before leaving the table top, continue the arc with "lead-pencil" upper arm and light, constant contact of fingers with the surface, and let all sorts of movement take place with forearm and hand. Keep the primary control with the "lead-pencil lever" — have constant progression with the drawing of the arc — while the forearm flexes, extends, and helps to propel the hand through its full capacity for lateral movement. Then try the keyboard, using a simple progression. (For example, a chromatic octave scale.)

III. (a) *Furnishing some power for tone production as progression takes place through several keys toward a destination;* or (b) *Taking control of the key-drop and producing the power for important tones:* It is easy to be aware of the delivery of power for tone when the upper arm takes full control of the key-drop, as it frequently does for important tones. It is much more difficult to sense its participation in the use of power for tone when there are multiple articulations going on as the upper arm moves to find the desired keys, constantly gauging the level at which power is delivered.

It is through maintaining the control for level that the power of the upper arm shares in the power for tone when multiple articulations are taking place. The greater the speed the more it can share (as in the ripped chord), but with octaves the speed of articulation is dependent upon a repeated action and determined by it, so the ripped chord becomes only good imagery for sensing the action of the first lever.

The first lever has a pattern of activity which is determined by the tones forming the musical idea and a destination determined by this musical idea. It must be adamant in continuing toward its destination (as with the glissando). Because of its capacity for many operations at the same time through the circular shoulder joint, no complication arises from its taking of the key-drop and using its power for full production of tone whenever there is an important tone to be stressed.

The "lead-pencil lever" draws one arc after another depending, of course, on the succession of keys the music calls for. It need never stop to begin again. It can round any angle and take the key-drop at any time it is propitious to do so.

There is only one value in describing a specific and detailed sequence of physical actions for playing a given musical example: It will show the reader how the over-all coordination may be applied to handle the technical problems successfully. It is not necessarily the only way; a performer's musical approach, plus his inherent capacity for speed, can change the details somewhat. But, being specific is helpful in establishing new habits, and, therefore, measure 9 of this Etude will be analyzed. This measure is chosen because octaves on consecutive white keys are always troublesome, and the reason they are troublesome is that playing them often encourages an imbalance of activity between the first-lever arc of progression and the levers used for articulation. A chromatic passage utilizes an in-and-out distance which quite naturally involves the arc of the upper arm. Consecutive white keys utilize a horizontal distance which tends to eliminate the arc of progression of the first lever and put in its place an added burden on the repeated action at the elbow. Top speed demands the ultimate in a balanced activity of the total playing mechanism. If that balance is disregarded or upset, for any reason, the passage will always remain troublesome.*

Allegro con fuoco   Op. 25, No. 10 (measure 9)

Ex. 4   a   b   c   d   e   f   g   h   i   j   k   l   m

One can play this example with the full-arm stroke. This serves both to get acquainted with the sound and to do this while making the upper arm active. If a student has enough training, and if his ears are good enough so that even the visual appearance of the page produces an auditory response, he can learn the music without ever playing it slowly. By outlining, first using very few notes of the measure (Ex. 4A) and adding a few notes at a time, a pianist can learn even a very difficult composition without ever playing it at any tempo other than the one which produces the excitement and pleasure of a musical performance.

4 A   a   m

* Abby Whiteside never did write a detailed analysis of this bar. Although we had decided to revise the original manuscript as little as possible, and not to attempt the analysis of the Etudes which she had not covered, it did seem to us that it would be useful at this point to show in some detail the means which were used to learn to play such a passage, and the reason why they worked. It seemed to be a good opportunity to show once again the manner in which outlining was to be used. [Eds.]

Swinging back and forth, with the upper arm describing a large, exaggerated arc, serves to make the upper arm active and to give both the ear and arm a destination. When this destination is vivid enough it is useful to lessen the arc until the elbow almost seems to be moving horizontally.

Example 4B hardly adds any complications. One should do this with the full-arm stroke; when the sensation is clear, change the motion so that it becomes what could be described as a snap of the forearm and hand by the upper arm — this involves flexing the forearm and hand while the upper arm is still involved in the slow lateral progression, plus an awareness of key level. A good physical image of what happens could be experienced by taking a towel and snapping it with both hands holding the towel. Note that this is no longer a full-arm stroke: The wrist is flexible, and the hand is readily flipped up and down.

These various examples of outlining, Exs. 4C, 4D, 4E and 4F, show how one adds the details in such a way as to preserve the drive and activity of the upper arm on its

way to a destination. Go back to the simpler versions
again and again, otherwise the added notes have a tendency to encourage the forearm and hand to overwork in
relation to the upper arm and thus jam the playing
mechanism. It is safe to say that every time the pianist
experiences difficulty, his upper arms are not sufficiently
involved in using a basic rhythm while the levers of articulation are working more than they should. It is ironic
that usually the pianist who is having this difficulty tries
to work all the harder with the levers of articulation —
the forearm, hand, and fingers. It is also true that some
of the difficulty comes from pressing hard against the
key bed, and that the more difficulty the pianist has the
harder he tends to press.

A particularly useful form of practice for measure 9 would be to transform this measure, every once in a while, into a chromatic progression: Ex. 4G. The in-and-out

4 G

motion which this chromatic progression stimulates in the upper arm should then be transferred to the passage as it is actually written. This Etude does not provide for as simple a physical analysis as Op. 10, No. 7. Flexions and extensions do not alternate with any systematic regularity; the musical texture does not provide for it. Remember that this is not an attempt at a definitive description which is the same for all pianists and all occasions. The individual physical characteristics of the playing mechanism of each pianist produce some variation in the actions involved and, for that matter, even any given pianist may have some variation in the spontaneous action of playing. What remains true for all pianists who do play this Etude with both beauty and ease is: There is an active upper arm which coordinates all other actions.

Example 4B — Octave *a* is played with the full-arm stroke, with the forearm and hand flexed. This would have the wrist high, which makes it easier to feel a bony alignment. The height is a relative matter; one can (and should) exaggerate when outlining: The time between notes permits it, but this action must lessen as one plays all the notes, because great speed does not leave room for exaggerated actions of articulation. Pianists can achieve their greatest speed only if the actions of articulation are at their minimum. Octave *g* can be played with an extension of the hand and forearm, while the upper arm stays poised and actively moving towards octave *m*.

Example 4c — *a* is played as before, but now *f* could be played with extension of hand and forearm and *g* would now be played with a flexion of the forearm and hand. The suggestion for playing *g* now differs from the earlier one (discussion of 4B). This is due to octaves *f* and *g* both being on white keys. It is just in such cases that the forearm can jam against the key bed; the alternating action (flexion and extension) of the forearm and hand helps to prevent this. Octave *i* can be played with an extension and *m* a flexion.

Example 4D — Only the last triplet presents something new. Octave *j* would be played with hand and forearm extended; the upper arm helps in reaching this by coming forward. By increasing the flexion of the forearm and hand as octaves *k* and *l* are played, a situation is avoided where an articulating lever, no matter how agile, is jammed by forcing it to play successive octaves by its own power.

When playing all the notes (Ex. 4), one would approach the first octave *a* with a full-arm stroke and forearm and hand flexed. Octave *b* would be played with an extension of hand and forearm, *c* by flexion once more. The first three octaves hardly call for any lateral distance; the next triplet would call for a slight turn of the humerus to reach the somewhat bigger lateral distance. One could again use a flexion of hand and forearm to play octave *d*, extension for *e*, a slight flexion for *f*, and increase the flexion for *g*; *h* — extension, *i* — flexion, and we are in position to reach the black-key octave *j* with an extension. It is possible to make one flexion cover two octaves: The flexion could increase from octave *k* to *l* and finally to *m*.

The above analysis underlines how varied the actions can be. The more the upper arm is in control the more spontaneous can be the various combinations of actions in the playing mechanism. The body has its own logic. Attempts to control precisely the various small actions will not stimulate the playing mechanism to greater virtuosity, but the very opposite. They will interfere with the natural coordination of the body.

The important over-all controls will be: upper arm, gauging lateral distance and, by means of the pull, controlling the actions of articulation; a snug forearm, an alert hand, picked up so lightly at the wrist that the slightest impulse of the upper arm and action of the forearm will throw it the way a whip is snapped, both through its up-and-down motion and the slight but essential lateral motion.

Etude, Op. 25, No. 12

This Etude will be discussed under five headings:

(1) Parallel Motion.   (2) Establishing a Basic Rhythm.   (3) Control of Distance.   (4) Power. (5) Detailed Analysis.

(1) Parallel Motion.

Parallel motion in single tones provides abundant opportunities to note that the action of the first large lever absorbs the multiple little actions involved in taking distance. Because the hands are opposite in the use of the same controls for covering horizontal distance, all the smaller actions are opposed to each other. Paying attention to these smaller actions, rather than the basic control, makes the achievement of top speed that much more difficult and often impossible.

There is a sweep up and down the keyboard by both arms, and the control of that sweep is a perfectly simple control at the shoulder. This shoulder control can be as simple as it is with the glissando, or almost as simple, if the details of precision for placement and articulation are properly related to this primary control.

This can be managed if sufficient time and attention is first given to the action controlling the sweep, before too much attention is given to the manipulation for controlling the details of placement. The sweep amounts to

nothing more than an easy swing to the right and back
again to the stance needed for the melody line. Pantomime the swing as though it were a way of using the
time between the melody tones. Repeat this swing in its
relation to playing the melody. Make it a swing which
is as smooth, as exactly timed between the melody tones
as the going-forward of the polo pony is between the contacts with the turf in the slow-motion picture. The relation of the sweep to the melody tones is the important
musical and technical factor in this Etude.

(2) ESTABLISHING A BASIC RHYTHM.

This Etude provides a clear and simple example of the
manner in which a basic rhythm is established. The action of continuity which produces the basic rhythm is
established by playing the melody tones and being involved in the swing between them.

There will be no better illustration — no simpler one
— of the relation of the basic rhythm to the steady progression of the musical statement, the form, than this
Etude provides. The torso quite naturally and simply
takes part in the swing up and down the keyboard but,
at the same time, constantly favors the playing of the
melody tones. That is to say, it will favor the melody
tones only if the pianist accepts the importance of simplicity in projecting the melody. The melody in this
case is formed most of the time by the progression of the
first tone of each measure. Thus there is in the torso the
action related to the entire playing, but with special
alignment for helping the melody on its way.

The mood is established by the desire to put forth a
sonorous melody, while feeling the excitement created
by the rhythmic sweep of the arpeggios. The activity
of the torso is always furthered by a good balance in sitting. This will mean using for resistance the ischial
bones, rather than the thighs against the edge of the seat
and the feet against the floor. There are several ways to
make one aware of this desired balance against the isch-

ial bones: Sitting cross-legged on the floor is one; sitting on one's hands on a chair and swaying gently in all directions is another.

Dealing with the musical statement always means dealing with the structural form of the composition. This feeling of form with the basic rhythm is insurance against a notewise procedure which is the deadly enemy of beauty and ease in playing. This calls for treating a composition as if the smallest musical unit is at least two measures long. So often the lack of grace in a musical performance is caused primarily by a measure-by-measure progression instead of one which uses a two-measure unit as the smallest base. Observe what happens in humming a familiar tune, how the dynamics are related to a two-measure unit and not a one-measure unit. Folk tunes are excellent for observing this relationship.

The opening of this Etude forms an eight-measure unit: two short two-measure units, balanced by a long unit of four measures. Establish a basic rhythm related to this eight-measure unit by playing the melody tones before giving attention to the details of playing the arpeggios.*

One of the attributes of the Chopin Etudes is the unrelenting use of one technical pattern for each Etude. When *con fuoco* is called for, any disturbance of the relationship in leverage for playing that technical pattern is sufficient to cause a lack of ease and grace in that particular spot. Accents outside the simple line can be used, but they must be tucked in on the way as the main line is adhered to. They must not usurp or interrupt the power of the large lever which is implementing the rhythm in the playing mechanism.

* A. W. is not recommending studying this Etude eight bars at a time. She simply means that a phrase-by-phrase progression must be established first. She felt very strongly that the best way to learn a composition was to play it as one unbroken unit, from beginning to end, rather than to study smaller sections and then string them together. [Eds.]

(3) CONTROL OF DISTANCE.

Here is an excellent opportunity for understanding the use of rotary motion as a factor in placing the hand in succeeding positions on the keyboard in relation to the repeated action for the same tone. Chord formation in the palm is emphasized because of the octave span and the repeated tones used in shifting the position of the hand along the keyboard, instead of passing the thumb under the hand, or the reverse, passing the hand over the thumb.

The analysis deals with the right arm; the left arm does exactly the same thing when it goes in the opposite direction. In short, the left arm goes through the same movements descending that the right arm uses ascending.

To make the presentation as simple as possible, no detailed analysis of distance separated from the use of power will be given. It is wise, however, constantly to bear in mind that the finding of the key — control of distance — comes first. It is the incorrectly handled control of distance which causes not only technical difficulties but even real strain. The sweep up and down the keyboard is controlled by the first lever. The forearm coordinates with the first lever and places the hand in its three registers by the use of the rotary action, plus some extension (on the repeated tones) going up the keyboard, and some flexion (on the repeated tones) going down.

Using the fifth finger and the thumb to play the repeated tones exaggerates the use of rotary action in this Etude; since rotary action is always a pertinent factor in arpeggio playing, watching it operate with even greater exaggeration is profitable. For this purpose, leave out the middle tone and use no adduction of the thumb while an untwist of the forearm bones is allowed to bring the thumb vertically above the little finger (the hand will be rolled over onto its side). Then with a twisting of the forearm bones, without any action on the part of the thumb, have the thumb contact the repeated tone by the movement of this twist. Fuss with this action until there is a clear realization of just how efficient the rotary action can be in placing the hand along the keyboard and sharing the action for taking distance with the thumb.

The musical pattern, by calling for the use of the fifth finger and the thumb on the repeated tones, is conducive to maintaining a sense of chord formation in the palm. Chord formation involves horizontal spacing of fingers and making their length "even" for the vertical distance from the palm to keys so that tones can be sounded simultaneously. It is very useful to play as if the palm is doing all the work for these two actions. The sensation of chord formation in the palm can be maintained even though there is some adjustment in the horizontal spacing if the fingers keep their even-length relationship from palm to keys. Maintaining the chord formation in the palm is a vital part of all easy arpeggio playing. It is a particularly useful tool for avoiding reaching with fingers, and anything which helps prevent that destructive habit is a great boon to facility.

Here again is an example of an action at center which moves in a small arc but produces a wider arc at periphery: A small contraction or expansion of the palm at its base will shorten or lengthen the distance of the span at the tips of the fingers.

(4) POWER: MULTIPLE ARTICULATIONS INSIDE OF A SIMPLE MELODY LINE — RELATION OF HAND TO FINGERS IN TAKING THE KEY-DROP.

The greater the responsibility given to the first lever, the greater will be the virtuosity in playing the arpeggios and the more easily will this virtuosity be achieved. This responsibility will include the initial control for all distance, a consistent, non-releasing control of the level at which tone is produced, an easy delivery of power for the melody tones as well as a definite proportion of the power for the arpeggio tones. This tremendously effi-

cient lever can accomplish all these controls simultaneously because of the many muscles acting through the
circular shoulder joint.

But its efficiency can be hampered, ruined in fact, if:
(a) the fingers reach for position and try to produce the
tone — their primary job is to stand alert under the power
of the upper arm and deliver this power to the key — or
(b) the activities controlled by the first lever (upper arm)
are ever released — the coordination of the arm as a whole
is cancelled. This release by the upper arm is always related to the fingers taking over controls which should not
belong to them. The in-and-out distance can be a pitfall
for the upper-arm power. The actions for taking it are
affected by the difference in distance between the body
and the black and white keys, and the difference in the
central operational points of the fingers (at the knuckles)
and the thumb joint (at the wrist) — the distance from
the knuckles to the wrist as opposed to the thumb joint
which is at the wrist.

An association between the control of in-and-out distance and the control of the level where tone is produced should become a habit. For the association of
these two controls use the imagery of the elbow as a large
"pencil lever" (see page 70). With the point of this "pencil," draw circles on a table top. Draw circles in all
directions. Keep the fingers in light contact with the
table surface and have a wrist so free that the circle drawing will move the hand constantly in all directions. The
elbow joint should be free also. And, *very important*,
move horizontally across the table while drawing the
circles. It is most important that a feeling of destination
— progression across the table and back again — is maintained, for otherwise each circle might become a separate
operation, an unrelated detail. Keep the sense of destination as strong as it is with the straight line of the glissando.

By the process of maintaining a strong destination plus
a consistent control of level, the circles or arcs needed for

the in-and-out distance need not disengage the muscular activity which produces the formidable power inherent in the use of the first lever. This power is in the nature of a pull. The pull gives a compactness to the entire body from ischial bones at chair seat to finger tips at keyboard, and this compactness in coordination is always in evidence when there is great speed.

(5) DETAILED ANALYSIS.

A detailed analysis need not be given for more than one arpeggio, but in actual practice use nothing less than a two-measure unit so there will be established the relation of melody tones. After all, it will gain us nothing to achieve the details if there is no form established to receive them, and the form lies with the progression of the melody tones.

Always practice with continuity, even though the continuity is with a repetition of the same pattern. Therefore, return to the first melody tone at the close of the second measure. Remember the difference in physical activity between placement and tone production. Placement always requires freedom at the wrist so that the hand may be propelled into position. Tone production uses the hand for taking part of the key-drop. That is, when the chord formation uses three fingers before the hand is propelled into a new register along the keyboard, and there are three separate articulations, the hand has a positive control of key-drop. One flexion of the hand produces the three articulations; this flexion at the wrist is coordinated with the pull of the upper arm by a flexion of the forearm.

The pull of the upper arm moves through a tiny arc of distance, maintaining the control of level — the forearm and hand extend the arc of distance. The forearm flexes (rises) to allow the flexion of the hand which is positive in taking part of the distance of key-drop as an extension of the upper-arm power. One flexion of the hand covers the articulation by the three fingers. The fingers do little more than vitalize to stand under the power, much as they do with a ripped chord.

With this flexion of the hand there is also a slight untwist of the rotary action which also shares in taking the key-drop. So by the time the third tone is played the hand has been slightly rolled over, the thumb has adducted slightly at the same time and is closer to the repeated tone next in line to be played. The rotary untwist will cause trouble if it is exaggerated. No more rotary should be used than will allow either the thumb or fifth finger to receive power from the arm. With rotary and thumb adduction there is also a shrinking of the width in the palm, and all of the actions are so blended and timed that not one of them can be isolated from the others. For the position of the repeated tone there is the "out" of the in-and-out distance. The elbow (pencil lever) starts drawing an arc, the forearm extends, the rotary untwists, and the hand is thrown out and over, so that the hand is over its new position. For the articulation of the thumb tone, the "pencil lever" is doing the "in" of the arc, the forearm is extending, and the rotary, by a retwisting, both shares the key-drop with the forearm, thumb, and upper arm and, at the same time, places the hand in its new register on the keyboard. The perfect timing of the untwisting and retwisting of the rotary action, as it places the hand in its new position, is of great importance. It means that with the playing of the thumb tone the hand is already in position for the new chord. See what would happen if a legato key-connection were tried for. The fifth finger would hold until the thumb goes to the key, and the new position of the hand would have to be taken after the thumb tone. Speed does not allow for any such waste in timing.

The same sequence operates for the third position up the keyboard, but something else occurs in this position because the direction will be changed to coming down the keyboard after the fifth finger is played. Here is an important point for all arpeggios which reverse their direction. The progression up the keyboard becomes a stance for the power with the playing of the thumb — a stance which allows for coverage with the power over the highest tone; actually the power has begun the shift in direction with the playing of the last high tone. If the power travels an infinitesimal distance too far up the keyboard before the turn, there will be difficulty with the first tones coming back. The power should never lose the sense of having the thumb available while the highest tone is being played.

When the power has an active stance with the fingers over the keys to be played and no progression to another octave, the fingers take a tiny amount more of the distance of the key-drop than when progression takes place, but always the action of the finger is timed to be a part of the activity of the whole arm.

Between the playing of the thumb going up and the thumb going down there is a rotary action which is exactly the same as when playing an octave tremolo. No

tremolo is easy if the power shifts at all from one side of
the hand to the other — too wide a rotary action will
cause this shifting. The power remains balanced sufficiently down the middle of the hand to be available to
both thumb and fifth finger. If the key is not allowed to
come up completely, the right balance for the octave
tremolo will be sensed. This same kind of balance will
help to make the turn from one octave to the next of this
arpeggio.

But now, with the direction down the keyboard, there
is not much rotary available; the pronation of the hand
for the playing position uses practically all of the twist
of the rotary action. The hand needs to be propelled
into position for efficient distance-taking since a replace-
ment is necessary for the easy untwisting of the rotary
which is available when one goes up the keyboard. There
is an extra turn of the humerus to lift the elbow; this
helps to tilt the hand toward the thumb and thus aid the
twist to cover the distance to the next octave. Do an
exaggerated twist away from the keyboard and watch
the contribution to its facility made by the position of
the upper arm.

The moment it has contributed resistance for the
power to be applied for its tone, the thumb releases at
the wrist joint along with the wrist release, while the
twist is bringing the fifth finger into playing position.
The importance of the freedom of the wrist cannot be
overestimated, because along with the twist, as stated
above, there is the adjustment at the shoulder and a
flexion at the elbow which propels the hand laterally and
drops it into position for taking the key-drop along with
the fifth finger and the untwist of the rotary. The moment that the time arrives for the fifth-finger tone, the
rotary by its untwist takes the key-drop and (this is very
important) throws the thumb out and levels the hand at
the same time for the new position along the keyboard.
What reads like a very complicated action becomes a
very simple one if nature is in charge of the coordination.

This means that the first lever draws a line which has a definite destination — the arrival at the melody tone — and the melody tones form by themselves another consecutive line.

Any consecutive line musically means a physical action of continuity, and only the actions at the shoulder joint can maintain continuity for more than one involvement in controls.

First, this upper arm is involved in making the musical statement; the power for the tones of this statement is delivered with the pull of the upper arm. Then, while the ear is dictating this tune, the upper arm turns slightly to control and gauge all distance for the arpeggio while it is delivering the power for tone, but it does this while keeping the melody going. Then it assists at all of the points where the hand must be propelled into position, and, for this action, in-and-out distance creates the need for some slight adjustment in and out.

All of the intricacies of adjustment will smooth out and get properly balanced in their give-and-take if the impulse for action, in response to the aural image, is in the upper arm and *not in the fingers*.

The parallel motion demands that the one simple control at the center of the radius of activity be the all-important control, and that the total coordination be achieved with perfect timing to this primary action.

A glance at what happens in parallel motion, when there is a finger control for finding the key and providing the primary power for taking the key-drop, is sufficient to prove the efficacy of one control (arms) rather than ten. Every control, if it is in the fingers, is opposite to the control in the other hand: Weak fingers play against the strong fingers; one hand passes the thumb under the palm while the other passes a finger over the thumb; rotary acts in opposing directions; flexion and extension of forearms are opposed. The whole process is enormously complicated and difficult. But a control by the first large lever lets both arms move in complete harmony without

competition or opposition. It modifies all actions automatically by the importance of its own action for the
sweep up and down the keyboard.

If observing is to be really instructive, watch what
happens to the upper arm and not the fingers. It is always possible to see that the big levers are very active,
and it is their activity which counts most in relation to
speed, brilliance, and ease. Great speed cuts down the
size of all movements. The detailed actions described
above cannot be seen, but if any movement which assists
in taking distance is omitted there will be immediate difficulty with the passage; arpeggios, with their width between keys, augment this difficulty.

Watching a pianist play this Etude with virtuosity
makes one realize that there must be an easy coordination
for playing it. That easy way always entails the complete balance in activity which nature alone can produce
when the first lever controls distance and power.

Constantly practice the melody line while pantomiming the sweep of the arpeggio. Then tuck in the last half of the measure, not paying as much attention to accuracy of details as to the uninterrupted arrival for playing the melody tone. Then tuck in a whole measure, but never

play the arpeggio before the melody has demanded continuity in progression. Never stop at the end of the
tucking-in process. Go right along, no matter what has
happened.

Never practice *stopping*. Practice *continuity* in action.
The arpeggio must conform to the playing of the melody,
and the melody must be played phrasewise — not notewise. So, heed well the basic rhythm. Practice using a
basic rhythm until it becomes all important in expressing your emotional reaction to this surging music.

Etude, Op. 25, No. 11

Here is an excellent illustration and proof that:

(1) Notewise procedure does not further bravura playing.

(2) Finger technique is simply not adequate for brilliance and speed.

(3) Any idea that keys should be connected by a legato while passing from one hand position to another is a fallacy, and a very hampering fallacy.

(4) The greatest assistance for securing the necessary coordination is a commanding rhythm.

The right hand has two tonal patterns which have to be solved before this Etude is playable. They are: the descending chromatic scale with a tone below the line of the scale tucked in after each scale tone; and a broken arpeggio at the end of this run.

The left hand has one difficult tonal pattern as exemplified in bars 17–18, but otherwise it is concerned with implementing the mood and the unrelenting pace of the basic rhythm.

The reader will learn a great deal about how parallel scales ought to be played if he will play the A minor scale at the end of this Etude after establishing a basic rhythm and while the mechanism for parallel arpeggios is still freshly in mind.

But first we must deal with the basic rhythm. The two-measure unit is clearly defined in the first four-measure opening phrase. In establishing the basic rhythm the torso facilitates and often augments the action of the first lever (upper arm). The torso is the fulcrum which gives the powerful upper arm its effective leverage. The upper arm, because of the circular structure of the shoulder joint, operates in all directions.

The torso, balanced against the chair seat, can sway in all directions and thus facilitates the taking of distance. It can also produce a bouncing movement by contracting and relaxing the muscles of the buttocks (the muscles between the ischial bones and the chair seat); and when the music progresses by a very commanding, rhythmic beat, the torso often uses this bounce to express the emotion produced by that resounding beat. The torso has capacity for flexibility in movement and thus the movement of the torso conforms to the flexibility of the music, as it expresses the mood which the music inspires.

The whole arm, by means of the consistent pull of the upper arm which controls and coordinates all the necessary activity, is an integrated part of the movements made in the torso, as an expression of the emotional reaction to the music. There is no division, no separate action in the reaction of the torso and the upper arm to the aural image. That is the thing to remember. There cannot be any movements which stress a notewise procedure if there is never any separation in emotional reaction between the torso and the upper arm. Neither the torso nor the upper arm can deal with all of the articulations of meter. They deal with the important beats of the meter, and the music manifests its form through these important beats.

The right arm makes the announcement of the first two-measure unit, and for that announcement there is just one strong beat — the first one. The rest glides off of that first beat with the smoothness of an airplane leaving the ground for its flight. What does that imagery suggest? It is hoped that it will produce in the reader, trying it out at the piano, a unified power of the upper arm and torso which plays the first tone and then, while this power is held suspended, the other articulations will be made by forearm and hand underneath the canopy of power by the pull of the upper arm with the accompanying activity of its fulcrum — the torso.

Then, without the stress of an accent but with an emotional intensity holding the power at strict attention, the second two measures are played in the same manner as the first two. Only there is the added intensity of holding produced by the retard and the fermata which indicate that something electrifying is about to happen. And it does happen, with a dramatic *sforzando* on the bass A which gives over the rhythmic form to the left arm and torso. The same four-measure phrase is now completed by an added four measures, and on, and on with no stopping of the activity in the torso and first lever.

Ends of phrases should not let down — they should carry over. Rests in the music are places to hold the power at attention — not for a release of power and a cessation of the rhythmic follow-through. Nothing is more harmful to a musical performance than letting each phrase die at the end. Retards are only vitally effective when they are played in such a manner that the audience waits with bated breath for what is about to follow. Only one retard should be final in its conception and that is the one at the close of the composition. Only a basic rhythm can make retards exactly right. If a retard is felt between articulations rather than as an extended holding of the phrasewise rhythm it will never have any convincing emotional quality.

The closing A minor scale is a dramatic extension of the last chord and rounds out the rhythmic form; do not feel that this scale is just tacked on after the chord. The chord cannot finish the composition until the phrase-form is completed and the scale sweeps to the finish of that time unit. The power which played the chord does not release but forms the sweep of the scale.

There is no difference between arpeggios and scales in the movements involved for each. There is only a difference in the arc of·the actions; the actions are smaller in width for the scale. But the fingers, when they have had specialized training, are so easily available in a diatonic progression that they are bound to take over a proportion of the controls for distance and power which does not rightfully belong to them. Then the entire balance of activity is destroyed and the scale loses much of its beauty in sweep and certainly loses much of the ease of production. Translating "beauty of sweep" into the medium of sound involves the kind of gradation in the use of dynamics which results when one power draws the line of progression which leads the ear forward inevitably.

At the root of much of the difficulty in scale playing is a conscientious key connection — legato in passing. It has been well 'emphasized in our traditional training, but it simply is no more true in virtuoso scale playing than it is true in playing arpeggios; and the analysis of the coordination to be used for playing the scale at the end of this Etude should prove conclusively the difference in ease between passing which gives over the responsibility to the large levers, and passing which involves key connection with fingers.

For this scale, as with the arpeggios of the Etude in C minor, Op. 25, No.12, two upper arms sweep up the keyboard. They hold their power channelled down the center of the hand so that it is available to all fingers all of the time; and they keep the control of level constantly. The fingers vitalize to receive the power initiated by the upper arms and transmitted and supplemented by forearm and hand.

The hand is propelled into position in exactly the same manner as was described for the arpeggios, and there is no attempt at legato in passing. All legato — the feeling of it — is in the sweep of the power up the keyboard. The sweep for this swift scale should be almost as strong as it is with a glissando; it is produced by the pull and slight turnings of the humerus, plus the torso adding its adjustment to distance and its steady holding as the fulcrum.

Refresh the sensation of the rhythm of form and, when

it is strongly felt, try for the coordination which will make measures 17–18 play inside that rhythm without their feeling impossibly difficult.

Ex. 8

The difficulty arises when the long line of rhythm is interrupted by a faulty manner of finding the keys. *Direction* is involved when these measures seem difficult; direction must always be right when skips and multiple articulations are involved. These two measures could be practiced weeks on end and never become secure if there is a faulty use of direction in progression. Also, the power must always be balanced — take its stance — in favor of the right articulations, or there will be difficulty with distance. Faulty direction causes difficulty with the distance and is always related to the stance of the power, but these are two separate factors.

Direction is used to mean distance up and down the keyboard. If the long line of progression is up the keyboard, the power cannot be turned down the keyboard to take some intervening articulations which lie below the primary tones used for progression. The difficulty for the left hand in bar 17 lies with the triplet and the rolled chord. The

long line of progression uses C, E, E-flat and the octave
C-sharp.

Ex. 9

The tempo is very fast. To make the first chord of the
triplet easy, the power (upper arm) must not be balanced
too far down the keyboard. Take a stance over the chord,
and then try playing the C of the triplet (and later B, C
of the same triplet) with forearm extension and rotary
action, plus the lateral distance being covered by the hand
propelled by the strong impulse of the forearm. Don't
lose the feeling that the chord is still available with the
arm power, because the power is going to need continuity
for going from the chord of the triplet to the E-flat of the
rolled chord of the fourth beat. In taking the stance for
the chord in the triplet, care should be taken to avoid any
sensation that the power is lined up with the thumb.
Rather, the power is lightly balanced over the fourth
finger (unless the hand is large, using the third finger on
the G of the chord doesn't help one to go down to the other
notes of the triplet at all).

It is quite amazing how much the sensation of great
width in a skip can be diminished if the power is balanced
in exactly the right spot to make it easy to reach the
lowest and highest tones.

From the chord of the triplet to the top three tones of
the rolled chord there can be no turning down the keyboard to get the B-natural, the C and the C-sharp of the
rolled chord. The power must be aimed to go from the
chord of the triplet to the top tone of the rolled chord,
and it can stand at attention on its way but it cannot be
changed in direction — it cannot go down to take the
lower tones. The stance of the power (upper arm) must
make those tones available by action of the forearm and
hand. Rotary and extension of the forearm make it pos-

sible for the hand to cover some lateral distance, and these actions have to tuck in the lower tones. The stance of the power is always determined by the availability of the rotary action. It is the untwist which is an enormous aid in taking distance; with the left hand that means that distance down the keyboard can use this untwisting action of the rotary.

Thus, the C on the first beat and the C-sharp octave on the fourth beat can be taken more easily away from the power stance favoring the chords than the chords could be taken from a stance favoring the C and the C-sharp octave.

Play the passage, omitting in the left hand the single tones of the triplet and the C-sharp of the rolled chord, until there is a flowing progression (Ex. 9A). Then tuck in the C-sharp of the chord (Ex. 9B) and later the C (Ex. 9C) and, last of all, the B-natural of the triplet (Ex. 9D). An easy speed becomes available if the *direction* and power stance are right, and the fingers do not interfere by reaching for the positions.

The broken arpeggio patterns (for the right hand) provide by far the greatest difficulties in this Etude; measures 17–18 use the same tonal pattern found in measures 9–10, but the change of key and the various intervallic changes exaggerate the movements involved in passing. They furnish, therefore, a better proof that legato in passing is a matter of handling dynamics rather than a matter of key connection. That is why we shall use measures 17–18 for the detailed analysis.

Fingering in most cases is not a vital problem — certainly it is never a primary cause of frustration in achieving success with a passage. It is always the reaching for position with the fingers, and not the specific choice of fingers, which is the great destroyer of ease. But here is an instance where a consistent relationship in the sequence of fingers is an important factor in producing facility. Except for the chromatic scale with its tucked-in tones and a few other places, the entire Etude has a pattern which quite logically uses the same sequence in fingers — namely 5, 2, 4, 1.

It does not pay to change fingering for a repeated tonal pattern in order to avoid a thumb on a black key, or for any reason related to legato playing. With this pattern and fingering 5, 2, 4, 1, a legato key connection in passing is quite obviously not possible, so it suits our needs for giving all possible proof that a legato key connection between consecutive groups of tones on the piano is not the basis for producing what we hear as legato playing in fluent passage work. It is always the manner in which dynamics are handled which produces the impression of a legato performance. Although the sequence in fingering is a four-tone pattern, do not lose sight of the fact that the music uses a six-tone group and also that the meter (according to some important sources) is *alla breve*, so there are only two beats to a measure.

Direction is a primary factor again. The long line of direction, up the keyboard or down, must have continuity in progression while the tones lying in the direction opposed to the long line are tucked in. The speed of progression of the power with the long line is always determined by how many tones lie between the tones which are the pivotal points for passing the hand, and what is the distance between keys for these tucked-in tones. In other words, that is how long the upper arm must maintain availability of its power for the in-between tones before it moves to the next position on the keyboard. It is helped on its way by a slight shifting in balance in favor of the passing to be accomplished; and its original stance over the tones to be played in one position (chord formation in the palm) is also always in favor of the long-line direction.

Thus we start with a chord formation of the first three tones with the power balanced as far over the fifth finger as is possible while still maintaining access to the second tone.

Ex. 10

Direction and the long line of progression are associated with the thumb in ascent and with the fifth finger in descent, for with their usage the hand is placed in its new position.

In-and-out distance is exaggerated in this tonal pattern because the thumb plays a black key. The black keys are farthest from the body, and the central thumb joint at the wrist is farthest from the keys. So the "pencil-lever" (upper arm) draws a rather sharp curve for its share of the in-and-out distance. This action is practically unnoticed as it takes the *in* of the in-and-out distance because of the pull of the lever as it assists in producing power for tone and the extravagant flexion of forearm and hand. There is some slight twist of rotary involved with playing the second finger, which immediately changes to an untwist for the fourth finger. To summarize, the playing of the first three tones is shared by the pull of the upper arm, the rotary action, the forearm, hand, and finger flexion.

The thumb's previous position was an octave away from the B-flat of the pattern being analyzed. While the first three tones are being produced, the thumb adducts comfortably and smoothly, without a sense of reaching for its position which could produce a sort of jerking it into position. The flexion of the forearm is enough to produce a high wrist and, with the untwist of the rotary, the thumb is approximately over G when the action for passing takes place.

Passing is always identical as to the movements involved, but the degree — largeness — of the movement varies. Going up the keyboard, the forearm extension and untwist of the rotary throw the hand into the new position. Here, these movements have to be large to get the thumb to the key it is to play.

Ex. 11

The taking of the key-drop for B-flat is largely accomplished by the pull of the upper arm, the extension of the forearm, and the retwist of the rotary. The thumb is an extension of these movements. The retwist of rotary is a miracle of efficiency for placing the hand in playing position for its new set of tones. With the passing of the thumb to the highest B-flat in the measure, procedure up the keyboard ceases, but if there is a feeling for the *alla breve* meter there is a strong sense of going forward with the power to the A on the second beat.

Ex. 12

This strong current will be felt if the upper arm takes the key-drop for the first tone of the measure, and swings along to repeat a similar control for the A of the second beat. Immediately, with the playing of the A in the middle of the measure, the upper arm goes forward to the first tone of the next measure, and so on. Along with taking full control for these tones on the beats, the first lever maintains its control of distance and level between the beats.

When the long line of direction goes down the keyboard the power favors the thumb in its balance to facilitate passing, and the balance toward the thumb begins instantly when the A has been played. Once again, if the same sequence in fingering is maintained, and if a legato, by means of an actual key connection is stressed, the passing will be completely unwieldy, if not practically impossible. Passing is always easy if the power travels smoothly and maintains the control of placement and level, and if the hand is propelled into position by the two large levers. The wrist can greatly facilitate or ruin easy passing down the keyboard in this pattern. The hand should do whatever it can to take lateral distance, to compensate for the lack in availability of the rotary action in coming down the keyboard. Unless the wrist is very free indeed the slight turn of the humerus to raise the elbow, thus facilitating the tilt of the hand toward the thumb, and the slight flexion of forearm, plus the twist of rotary, will still not manage to propel the hand into position. At any rate, it is much more difficult to teach the lateral throw of the right hand down the key board, than to teach the lateral throw up the keyboard

Ex. 13

The broken arpeggio downwards, in bar 17, provides an excellent pattern for finding out just how important

it is that the hand be propelled into position. The upper
arm, forearm (flexion and rotary), and the hand bring the
fifth finger into position. The key-drop for A (marked
with an asterisk) is taken by the pull of the upper arm,
flexion of the forearm and hand, the untwist of rotary and
the vitalization of the fifth finger; flexion of the forearm
makes flexing the hand possible. Rotary action plays
an important role in the leveling of the hand for playing
in its new position.

If these details are accurately timed with the progression
of the first lever, and this lever keeps its control of distance
and level, there will be no consciousness of any break in
the legato when the hand is passed to the new position on
the keyboard. The whole passage will flow smoothly and
easily, but will always be impossibly difficult if fingers
take over the finding of the key and try for a key connection in passing.

The chromatic scale with its tucked-in tones, measures
5–8, is only difficult when there is a notewise procedure
and the rotary action is too large. A notewise procedure
means a fresh initiation of power for each tone; this
creates notewise listening. Fingers which do too much,
and a rotary action which is too wide will create this
faulty result: The ear listens primarily to each tone, as
it is produced, instead of listening ahead to the conclusion
of the musical statement. A glissando illustrates what
is meant by the ear going ahead. The destination in a
glissando is so demanding that the ear is forced to attend
to it and, with one power producing all of the tones, the
ear is not tempted to listen to each tone, but goes as the
power does — from start to finish, with the middle tones
played on the way to the finish.

The cure for notewise playing in any passage is an
emphasis on the basic rhythm which deals with the
musical statement as a unit. So, establish vividly the
basic rhythm, let the mood of the music run through
your ears and body, and then play the chromatic scale,
using the fingering necessary for the playing of all the

tones of the pattern. Make music with this scale — have it run its course from beginning to end as a part of the dramatic rhythm of the bass. Draw a line with the "pencil-lever" which runs through all of the tones with a strong feeling of progression toward the completion of the four-measure phrase. Then tuck in the tones which lie between the tones of the scale.

Ex. 14

The power favors the scale line in balance so that these tones can flow as easily as if there were no other tones to be played; but the power does not balance so far over the fifth, fourth, and third fingers that it must shift in balance in order to be available for the second finger and the thumb. A shifting of balance happens if the rotary action is too large, and the result would be an interruption of the scale, a notewise procedure, and no easy velocity.

With the power balanced approximately over the fourth finger, the scale is played with the pull of the upper arm and flexion of the forearm, hand, and fingers taking the key-drop and furnishing the power for tone. The rotary action places the fifth finger in its various positions and also furnishes a good bit of the vertical distance for the tucked-in tones; the fingers furnish the rest. Establish the sensation of progression with the scale and maybe halfway down tuck in the other tones. If there is difficulty starting the arpeggio at the finish of the chromatic passage, the chances are great that it will be caused by a faulty control of distance and faulty direction.

Faulty distance is always a possibility — fingers try to help out, and then the activity of the entire coordination is thrown out of balance. Faulty direction means that the power continues to travel down the keyboard a bit too far before the turn in direction takes place. But the main difficulty with this Etude comes from too much activity by the fingers; the reverse side of that picture is an insufficient amount of control in the two large levers.*

* At this point it seemed to us essential to show again in some detail how a basic rhythm can be established. A brief two-measure excerpt is used for the sake of convenience to show procedures which are to be used in learning the Etude as one continuous and uninterrupted musical form. The only exception to such a procedure in A. W.'s teaching was the recommendation that, in order to set up an active basic rhythm, the first two measures be played over and over without stopping, using various forms of outlining, before going on to play the rest of the composition.

This Etude provides another example, so frequently found in these Etudes, of a composition in which the form is clearly present in one hand while the other has most of the difficulties. Even very gifted students, during the years when they are learning to play the Chopin Etudes, frequently lavish all their care on solving the problems of the difficult hand while neglecting the hand which contains the primary musical statement. As a result, one of the commonest experiences in the concert hall, during a performance of an Etude, is hearing one hand played in a scintillating manner while the other one is insensitive and pedestrian. The technical problems have been solved — the music has been lost.

Abby Whiteside says, " ... establish vividly the basic rhythm, let the mood of the music run through your ears and body ... "; these are not two separate activities. Her experience as a teacher led her to the conviction that the body coordinates in a different manner when the emotions are involved than when they are not. Because the ultimate goal is, obviously, to have as compelling a statement of the music as possible, practice will be more to the point and effective if it always involves the emotions.

Letting the music run through one's ears and body implies knowing the sound of the music. At the beginning of this study she dealt both with those who, because of excellent ears, could immediately translate the printed symbols on the page into sound, as well as those who had to work harder to achieve this. Nonetheless, even before the music is thoroughly known, one can establish a rhythm more easily by making the left hand the starting point. Setting up a balanced stance on the ischial bones, one lets the music course through one's ears and sways in response to the aural image. At first, it is good to use an exaggerated swaying; as the mood becomes pervasive, one lessens the sway until, in some cases, it becomes almost invisible to the eyes of another person. In short, one should never start playing until the rhythm of the music is running through one's ears and body like a purring, warmed-up motor. [Eds.]

One of the most helpful ways to establish a rhythm in this Etude is to play the left hand part with both hands. This has a way of involving the pianist's complete attention and setting up a balance between the arms. Beginning with an outline helps to establish an awareness of the large form. As one continues outlining repeatedly, the omitted notes are tucked in gradually so that this awareness of the large form is preserved right along, with a strong sense of momentum as the performance takes shape.

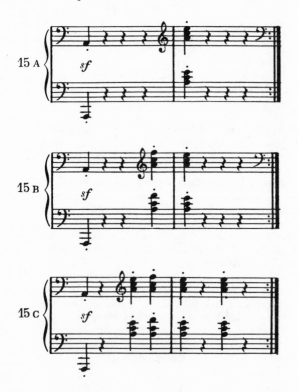

Then add some of the notes of the scale (possibly in octaves).

When the basic rhythm produces a strong enough drive forward, one might try blocking the actual notes; always omit any notes which threaten to hamper this drive and revert to a simpler, more basic, structural statement.

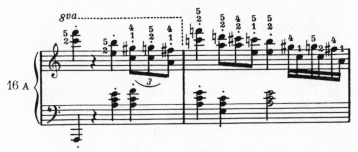

The examples of outlining provided here are but a few of the many possibilities. It is also useful to play the entire chromatic scale, either in octaves or in two-note blocks, before opening the pattern for playing all the notes.

Work Sketch for the Chopin Etudes, June 13, 1953

❧❧

GENERAL INTRODUCTION

Performance includes:

(1) The aural image of the music.

(2) The physical actions for producing tone.

(3) The physical actions for producing the rhythm of form (phrase-by-phrase sequence) and the rhythm of meter (note-by-note sequence).

(4) The physical actions which express the emotional reaction to the music.

A superlative performance includes:

(1) A perfect aural image — absolute pitch.

(2) Creative ideas.

(3) The rhythm of form associated with all the physical actions for tone production.

(4) The emotion expressed through the actions involved in producing the rhythm of form — not with the rhythm of meter.

This analysis will deal with the physical aspects of playing the Etudes: the actions involved in controlling distance, tone production, producing a rhythm, and expressing emotion.

There can be failure to understand the analysis on two scores: The analysis may not make all the points sufficiently clear, or the reader, possessing established habits for playing which have conditioned both his listening habits and his conclusions as to how the instrument is played, cannot completely realize the imagery of words and thus be stimulated to the right physical action. Established habits cannot be effaced at will, and they greatly retard the acquiring of new habits.

So long as a difficult passage remains difficult, the cause lies in faulty habits of tone production. The minute that the efficient and right coordination takes place the difficulty disappears. But until the actual *sensation* of the right adjustment takes place there is no way of being completely aware of what is faulty and what is right.

Take, for instance, just one of the many habits which can block the understanding of the elements which produce a top performance: The combination of perfect pitch and, predominantly, a finger technique for producing each tone will almost certainly result in a notewise listening habit. The ear will focus attention on the pitch of each tone as it is produced. This is a murderous habit for ever being able to produce a phrase worthy of distinction. It is akin to the telling of a story, stressing the unimportant as much as the important words.

The only remedy I have found for this notewise listening habit is to establish the physical habits for producing a phrasewise rhythm. That will take constant attention for a considerable span of time.

Unfortunately, a written analysis must deal first with one ingredient and then another, although the one aim of this analysis is to give an awareness of the complete coordination of the body as a tool for making music. Never lose sight of the fact that an isolated control is a hindrance and not an asset for actual playing. Only a rhythm of form can throw the entire mechanism into gear.

Each Etude simply highlights one aspect of the technical equipment; each Etude uses all of the equipment all the time. Turn from one to another and the pattern changes, as with a turn of the kaleidoscope a new design appears, but the ingredients remain the same.

A very special ingredient is the projection of the emotional reaction to the music. A performance is worthless without it. The entire musculature changes when the emotions are involved. Routine drill of mechanics excludes this emotional factor. Practice perfects only the elements in use. Why not consistently practice using the complete tools needed for an arresting performance. No other kind of practice is adequate for developing the full potential capacity of the performer, and routine practice may very easily balance the odds against the exciting performance.

Consistently practicing with all the tools necessary for perfecting an exciting performance means one thing: The projection of emotion (the actions which express it) must be channeled with the rhythm of form.

If this rhythm of form is the one factor which can throw the switch for a complete coordination of the mechanics needed, and if it can be made to channel the emotional output, then installing this rhythm of form is *the* primary requisite of every performer's training.

Without the rhythm of form, the action which deals with the relation of phrases, there are left only the actions which deal with the production of details. If the emotional output is involved with the actions dealing exclusively with the production of details, then details will be more important than the expression of the coherent musical thought. It is like telling a story with too much stress on modifying clauses — the meaning becomes blurred.

The badge of all inadequate performances is emotional intensity expressed with details (the rhythm of meter) taking precedence over the flow of ideas (the rhythm of form).

To play the Etudes at a professional level of speed and brilliance involves the physical actions which produce and control:

I. Rhythm.

    (*a*) Rhythm of form — the emotional reaction expressed with rhythm of form.

    (*b*) Rhythm of meter — the contacting of all tones.

II. All distance — horizontal, vertical, in-and-out.

III. Power for tone.

Even if it were possible to give the full details of actions made in order to accomplish a completely successful performance, it would be unwise to try to do so. The most effective analysis is the one which highlights the activity that initiates the controls which will insure full use of all the resources necessary for a superlative performance, and thus establish a picture which will be both simple and cohesive.

For the sake of clarity, from now on the word *rhythm* will be used to mean rhythm of form; rhythm of meter will always be labeled as such.

I. RHYTHM.

A. Attributes are:

1. *Destination* — the completion of a musical idea. The simplest physical demonstration of this is to play a glissando. In the Etudes, it is the end of each Etude which is the destination. Means of arriving at the destination: phrasewise rather than notewise progression.

2. *Continuity* in the movement toward the destination — like the action one sees in a slow-motion picture — is the life blood of a rhythm. This continuity refers to what the pianist does in-between the actions of striking keys.

B. Movements *implementing* a rhythm are initiated by action in the torso and augmented by the torso.

Movements *expressing* emotion are initiated by action in the torso and transferred to the playing mechanism by the upper arm.

Tools for Creating a Rhythm — the Upper Arm
Plus the Torso

All muscles exert their power by means of the bony structure of the body.

The arm is dependent for power upon the torso which acts as its fulcrum.

The arm is attached to the torso through a circular joint which allows continuity in action, and action in all directions.

The torso is balanced upon the two ischial bones against the chair seat; the power of its muscles acts against the resistance of the chair seat. Continuity in action is possible for the torso through the shifting of balance from one ischial bone to the other.

The Upper Arm

Unless the movements of the upper arm have a positive part in the production of *all* tones, there is no chance for the rhythm to influence the dynamics of tone production. Without the presence of a basic rhythm with its *continuous* power which is tone-producing, there is no chance for dynamics to be used with the subtlety in gradation which is necessary for creating a musical statement of astonishing beauty, such as is produced by a great artist.

For the moment, imagine the arm as a three-section telescope, and, in order to focus attention on the activity and controls of the upper arm, place the hand, palm down, on the shoulder and imagine the forearm and hand telescoped into the upper arm so that only the large section remains. Place the tip of the large section — the elbow point of the upper arm — on a table top (at a height which does not create a strained position) and treat the table top as a keyboard. The surface of the table top becomes the level of the key bed — the bottom of the key-drop. While tone is produced just before the key bed is reached, this level of key bed, where resistance to the application of power becomes definite, can be used efficiently for the delivery of power, providing there is full realization that the power used for tone production never continues to press against this key-bed level. It does one of two things: Either it moves on to the next tone with an evenness in procedure such as is seen in the slow-motion picture or, as in the production of speed (a glissando illustrates action of fast procedure), it hovers against the key with just the minimum of power to prevent the key from coming up (like the humming bird poised in the air).

Describe all kinds of figures on the table top with the point of the elbow without breaking the line of procedure; maintain constant contact with the table top, the level for tone production.

A well-trained hand is an incredibly persistent block in the way of achieving a definite physical sensation of the controls which rightfully belong to the upper arm. When new habits of performance are desired, imagery is a potent assistance. Use imagery to negate hand activity and emphasize the activity of the upper arm.

The imagery of telescoping the arm leaves only one shaft — the upper arm. Now, imagine the fingers appearing at the end of that single shaft. The contact with the table top will produce a line for each finger as the elbow point moves smoothly toward a destination point. Or, movement toward the destination can proceed as a bubble moves — touching the table top and veering and touching it again — each touch making five dots, but without stopping to make the dots. The five dots will become five key depressions, five tones produced when the finger tips contact the key bed.

If a rhythm becomes the most potent factor in the playing mechanism, the result will be activity by the upper arm, which is tone-producing, with a strong sense of progression. Progression, constant activity with the upper arm, is not produced by a simple action of one restricted type such as that produced at a hinge joint. Progression involves multiple, infinitesimal *turnings*, like the shifting of the eyes to include seeing a different area. Becoming conscious of these turnings of the humerus at the shoulder joint implies an increase in one's awareness of the major portion of the activity which produces a rhythm in playing. Examine these turnings while the upper arm is producing a variety of patterns on the table top.

The Torso

The torso is a fulcrum for the power of the upper arm. It expresses the mood of the music created by the emotional reaction to the music.

The torso, functioning as the fulcrum for the activity of the upper arm, needs consideration only to insure that it possesses an easy equilibrium upon the ischial bones as it rests on the chair seat. This balance makes for a constant, complementary, follow-through movement of the upper-arm action. One can imagine a torso well grounded and immobile while the arm plays, but one never sees such a torso when the artist plays. Instead, the moment that the aural image dictates action for producing tone, the torso becomes alive as though a current of electricity has been turned on — as indeed it has been — the current of emotion.

A properly balanced torso not only compounds the power of the controls initiated by the upper arm, but is also an efficient saver of energy. To achieve a well-balanced torso sit on the floor cross-legged. Immediately, the weight of the torso is balanced on the ischial bones, and the thighs are free of pressure. If the torso is not balanced against the ischial bones when sitting on a chair there will be pressure on the thighs. That pressure means that the torso is off balance, and only muscle energy is keeping the torso erect. Muscle energy should be conserved for tone-producing activity and should be used as little as possible for keeping the bony frame balanced and erect.

The torso, as related to the expression of emotion, is

the life saver of the rhythm. The actions which express emotion (usually labeled mannerisms) can be, and frequently are, the decisive factor which either helps the performer create a penetrating understanding of a composition, or warps the *structure* of the composition by placing the emphasis on details. How important physical actions are in determining the quality of a performance — in creating a mood — can be realized by trying to *feel* an adagio while dancing a gay waltz. It *can't* be done. The physical actions of the waltz will dominate the mood.

Two rhythms are always in operation in creating a composition: the rhythm of form and the rhythm of meter. Two rhythms must be in operation in creating a performance. The actions which express emotion will throw the balance of importance to one rhythm or the other. Exaggeration will take place either with the actions of articulation, or with actions related to the production of form. If the actions of articulation are made emotionally important the performance will be cluttered with far too many explosions. If the actions which produce the awareness of form are emotionally important the performance can unfold with simplicity and grace. They assure a performance which will deal with musical ideas rather than with exaggerated details.

The torso cannot produce the actions for taking the key-drop, the actions of articulation which produce the rhythm of meter, but it can and should produce the actions which stress the procedure by ideas, the rhythm of form, and the actions for expressing emotion with the rhythm of form. These actions, which are the outlet for emotional expression, can be small or exaggeratedly large. They are as varied as the personalities which produce them. The torso will sway, twist and turn, bounce up and down, or simply have an intensity of steady "holding the reins", as it were. It does not matter which actions are used; what matters greatly is that the torso does something which gives vent to the emotional reaction to the music. The torso must assist in creating the rhythm of form, in intensifying progression based on a relationship of musical ideas in order to avoid both listening and performing which is based on a notewise progression.

The manner in which a rhythm is dealt with determines the quality of a performance.

II. Distance.

The manner in which distance (the finding of the key) is controlled determines the ease in playing. If a passage feels difficult the chances are about one hundred percent that the fingers, rather than the upper arm, are in control of distance. Of necessity, the action for *finding the key* starts the entire playing mechanism which produces the tones in response to the aural image. Virtuosity in playing must necessarily involve all possible action operating together to cover distance — horizontal, vertical, and in-and-out.

If the initial action for finding the key is at the center of the radius of activity of the arm, it automatically can involve all the possibilities of action by all the levers.

The movement of the torso is always related to horizontal distance, but, since the activity of the torso is related to an area of the keyboard rather than any one key, its action is not included among the controls for distance. However, unless the torso does play an active part in the coverage of horizontal distance there will be difficulty with speed and accuracy in wide, horizontal distances. Thus there is, as it were, a second center of activity (second to the upper arm) for the control of horizontal distance — the torso.

A. *The Upper Arm:*

    (1) Moves in any direction by the turning of the humerus in its circular joint at the shoulder.

    (2) Can control the vertical action by pulling toward the torso.

(3) Adjusts, by a turn, the forearm for action in any plane from vertical to horizontal.

B. *The Forearm* possesses two kinds of action:
  (1) Flexion and extension in one plane through the hinge joint at the elbow (alternating action).
  (2) Rotation — twisting (pronation) and untwisting (supination).

Both extension and rotation can take the vertical* action which depresses the key — takes the key-drop. Flexion, extension, and rotation also can cover horizontal distance.

C. *The Hand* moves in all directions:
  (1) Can take vertical action — take the key-drop.
  (2) Moves sidewise for horizontal distance.
  (3) Can cover in-and-out distance by flexion and extension.

D. *The Fingers* move in all directions:
  (1) Flexion is available for taking the vertical action of the key-drop.
  (2) Flexion and extension share coverage of the in-and-out distance.
  (3) Sidewise action forms spacing for chord formation — horizontal distance.

E. *The Thumb* moves in all directions freely:
  (1) Because its large action is at the wrist joint, and that joint is on the average about four inches back of the first joint of the fingers, its coverage for in-and-out distance is small.
  (2) Through abduction and adduction, its coverage of horizontal distance is wide, in comparison to that of the fingers.
  (3) It can take the vertical action of the key-drop.

To summarize, controls of distance are:
  Upper Arm: Vertical, horizontal, in-and-out.

* See pp. 32 and 46.

Forearm: Vertical, horizontal.
Hand: Vertical, horizontal, in-and-out.
Fingers: Vertical, horizontal, in-and-out.
Thumb: Vertical, horizontal, in-and-out.

Important Combinations for Coverage of Distance

1. Horizontal Distance:
   (a) For large skips: Upper arm turns, forearm extends and flexes.
   (b) Coverage for arpeggios and scales: Upper arm turns; forearm flexes and extends; hand, fingers, and thumb move sidewise.
2. Vertical Distance of Key-Drop:

Upper arm pulls; forearm extends and flexes (the latter to allow flexion of hand); hand and fingers flex; the thumb adducts.

3. In-and-out Distance:
   (a) In-distance: Upper arm pulls; forearm and hand flex.
   (b) Out-distance: Upper arm moves toward keyboard; forearm and hand extend.

III. POWER.

Observe the use of the power of the arm in relation to daily living. Note that the most delicate operations always involve an alert control for action by the entire arm; this power is dependent for its effectiveness on its fulcrum, the torso. This should help to prove that it is incorrect to believe that the fingers, used independently, produce a greater subtlety in control than the entire arm does.

Power is generated by a contraction of muscles.

Bones furnish the resistive force which makes the muscle-action effective.

Tone is produced through a vertical key-action.

A down-action articulates tone.

Each lever of the arm possesses the capacity for a

down-action. The forearm possesses two down-actions: extension and rotation.

Articulation of tone is dependent upon the control of distance — finding the key. Control at the center of the radius of activity, the shoulder joint, is an indispensable asset for accuracy with speed.

Rhythm is dependent upon the manner of tone production: The continuity of action of the upper arm is an indispensable factor.

Producing successive tones with the utmost sensitivity in gradation of dynamics is dependent upon one large movement producing successive tones. The rhythm of form is essential for the kind of control subtle gradation in dynamics requires.

The coordination of these indispensable attributes of playing lies in acquiring activity in the upper arm as the first response for producing the tone imaged by the ear.

The knack of having some of the tone-producing power of the upper arm used for all tones all of the time is the secret of a technique which is adequate for virtuosity.

For the sake of simplifying and highlighting the delivery of power, we shall consider the key bed as the level where tone is produced. Actually, tone is produced by the time the key bed is reached, but just a flash before. It is by the consistent and continuous gauging of this level of key bed with the upper arm that all tone production is shared by the upper arm.

Some kind of action by the other levers, which lie between the upper arm and the key bed, is required to implement the action of the upper arm in tone production. Perfection in timing these actions is indispensable for a coordinated action by the total equipment for tone production. Coordinated timing for the use of power always acts from center to periphery, and such a coordination is the prerequisite for a superlative performance — whether playing the Etudes or, let's say, pole vaulting.

A five-tone chord,* played fortissimo and with the upper

* A. W. is referring to the tone-cluster C, D, E, F, G.

arm controlling the key-drop and power, uses the entire equipment, but does not involve the art of timing the use of all levers. One of the natural, automatic attributes of the adjustment for chord playing is an equalization of the five fingers in length as they stand under the palm. The tones must sound simultaneously — one lever puts all five fingers down — as the handle of a rake manipulates the teeth, because the teeth are attached to a bar and they are equal in length. The hand becomes the bar, and the fingers (the teeth) are equalized in length, for a concerted action dominated by one lever.

Now play this five-tone chord as loud as possible and see how adequately the bones of the fingers stand up under the application of that power. Then produce the same tones consecutively by ripping the chord with speed and power, using a pull towards the torso with the upper arm; there is in this operation a relationship between the action of the upper arm, forearm, hand, and fingers which should be used in all playing. There will be a shift in the *proportion* of action by the various levers for the different Etudes, but there should never be a shift away from the central control for the *initiative* of finding the key and producing the power for tone.

However, when the habits of tone production have been located in the forearm, hand, and fingers there is every reason to be suspicious that the fortissimo tones are not being produced by the upper-arm power. *And unless and until there is full control of key-drop by the upper arm, there will not be full control of the power for tone by the upper arm;* in such case none of the sequence of events — coordination *by the upper arm* of the various levers of the entire arm for production of tone — can be fully realized. In this simple fact lies the possibility of success or failure in playing the Etudes.

Unfortunately, there is no easy way of becoming aware of this control. It will take the utmost concentration on awareness of activity, plus good imagery, plus transferring the sensation of a simple act — such as pulling down a sticking window — to the keyboard, plus constant repetitions of playing the chord to make sure that the habits of production allow the upper arm to exercise its rightful role as the center of the controls, and, thus, control the key-drop and the power for tone at will.

With the upper arm controlling the key-drop and the power for the fortissimo chord, it is a simple step to rip that chord so that the tones sound in fast sequence rather than simultaneously.

Procedure for Ripped Chord (*ff*)

Ripping in contrary motion — from thumb to fifth finger.
Ripping in contrary motion — from fifth finger to thumb.
Ripping in parallel motion — up.
Ripping in parallel motion — down.

For full efficiency in using the ripped chord as a model for coordination for brilliant passage work, it is essential that the upper arm gauge the level for tone as it did for the fortissimo chord, when all the levers were in fixed position. That means there is no active down-pressure with either the forearm or the hand; both feel light, as if tipped up while the upper arm tips down. It also means that an exaggerated rotary is not used in the rip from the thumb to the fifth finger.

The benefits of using this procedure (ripped chord):

(1) Ripping a chord with great speed and brilliance causes so much power to be delivered by the upper-arm pull that the action by the other levers is scarcely discernible; only the one strong movement of the pull is felt; one strong pull plays five tones.

(2) The power of this pull is used at the bottom of the key-drop, at key-bed level.

(3) The entire arm feels in one piece — one bone, as it were, from shoulder to finger tip at the moment power is used against the resistance of the key bed.

(4) This pull by the upper arm automatically uses expert timing — the hand does not reach the key bed ahead of the upper-arm pull.

(5) In spite of the fact that there is variation in action by the forearm, hand, and fingers for the various rips, *there is no change in the dominance of the sensation that one action, the pull, produces the five tones.*

(6) The fingers have no feeling of being ready for individual, independent action but, rather, have the feeling of the adjustment used for chord playing — a concerted action; this means a kind of snug sensation at the first knuckle.

(7) Extravagance in the use of rotary action disappears when the two arms are used in parallel motion; this is pertinent evidence that the habits best adapted for furthering the development of rhythmic sensitivity are habits which further the feeling of two arms acting as a unit, and not the habits which further a feeling of two arms which are separate in action.

Ripped-Chord Coordination for Playing Largo and Forte

The ripped-chord coordination is also used while playing *largo* and *forte*. The slow-motion picture is the best possible illustration of what will take place. The action of the jack rabbit, running at normal speed, looks like a series of bounces. Slow the picture down and, instead of seeing a bounce, one sees the most beautiful, flowing continuity of a slow, graceful action.

The essential fact to keep in mind is: Though the tempo changes from *presto* to *largo*, the action *can* and *must* remain the same. The relationship in the actions of the levers, where the controls are, remains the same. This is true if one believes that it is desirable to cultivate habits required for speed, rather than to cultivate habits which interfere with speed. Integration, not independence in action of the levers of the arm, is required for speed.

Spend hours cultivating independence of action, and the net result will be the formation of habits which are not geared for speed.

In slow motion we see all the actions which are also used for speed. What are these actions? They involve:

(1) Upper arm.
(2) Forearm.
(3) Hand.
(4) Fingers.

Keep in mind the imagery of the rake. The upper arm is the handle. The handle makes one slow, raking motion, slow enough to include five separate, little mounds of grass. The contact with the ground (key bed) is made for the first pile of grass, and the rest of the raking motion (the pull) keeps contact with the ground and picks up the other four little piles of grass (D,E,F,G) as it comes to them. Remember, it can't pick them up until it does arrive where they are. There is space between the piles of grass, but not so much space but that one rake — one pull — can cover the distance. Note that with the long, slow pull of the rake the upper arm swings back. The elbow (in other words, the upper arm) is lifted in any direction which facilitates the pull.

All the problems of coordination multiply the moment that horizontal distance is small (the distance between consecutive keys) and the time unit is long between tones (*largo*).

There is a reason why speed in performance elicits enthusiastic applause from the audience, while most *largo* playing produces only boredom. Listeners are only captivated when they are caught up by an eagerness to hear the completion of a phrase, an anticipation of what is coming. Anticipation is created by the manner in which rhythmic nuances and subtlety in dynamics are used with successive notes.

Only a rhythm can produce that subtlety. Only continuity in action can produce a rhythm. Continuity in action is only possible with the upper arm.

The upper arm never makes direct contact with the keyboard. When it is in complete control of the key-drop and power for tone, the forearm, hand, and fingers serve as an alerted, bony extension of the upper arm.

The great problem for virtuosity and projection of beauty in performance is to have the upper arm maintain a positive control of distance and power, with the forearm, hand, and fingers extending this control by actions which share in the coverage of distance and the delivery of power for tone; this problem is much more acute in slow playing.

All movement of the upper arm is made by the turning of the head of the humerus at the shoulder joint. We are so habituated to the superlative efficiency of this joint that we are quite unaware of its multiple turnings and its enormous delicacy in control. That is why imagery is so helpful in getting results. Use imagery and then observe the results in action. What is desired is the knowledge (an approximate one — complete knowledge is just not possible) of the relationship of movement of the upper arm to forearm, hand, and fingers.

It is this basic relationship and the timing of these actions which matter; it is not the specific amount of a specific action that matters. The picture seems clear as this relationship is set forth. One has only to play a pattern with both arms in parallel direction to observe an adaptation in all the related movements, because both the hands and rotary action are opposite in their greatest, natural efficiency when at the keyboard. What is the easiest relationship for one is not the easiest for the other. This is a powerful and convincing reason why an active control by the large lever (the upper arm) is vastly more efficient in creating virtuosity.

The best imagery I have found for helping to sense this relationship is the manner in which the lariat is controlled. The variety of forms made at the loop is controlled at will by a constant and consistently steady pull of the arm, as it *twists* and *turns* to gauge and produce the various forms at the loop. Suppose the lariat is to be placed "around" (over) five keys: The *pull* will make the lariat twirl to fit over those keys. The twirl changes the swing of the rope between the end, which is held, and the loop. The pull which produces the five tones changes the relationship of the forearm, hand, and fingers between tones. Through the continuous pull of the upper arm the changing relationship of the forearm, hand, and fingers produces a flow of action which fills the unit of time between the articulations of tone.

If a rhythm (a basic rhythm which is the response in the body to the rhythm of form of the composition) is conceded to be the prime factor of coordination for superlative playing, the importance of continuity in action between the articulations of tone must be recognized as a constant and vital factor in performance.

Performance is dependent upon the manner in which nuances of time and dynamics are used. There is no nuance worthy of the name which is made on a note-to-note basis; a sensitive modeling of a phrase can only be made through a strong sense of being on-the-way to the close of the phrase. There is no chance of achieving the utmost sensitivity in the use of dynamics and nuances of time except as a rhythm is functioning. Thus, the activity between tones is a necessity for sensitive modeling with the two essential factors of performance (timing and dynamics). The between-tones activity must be a consistent part of production for beautiful, slow playing.

Review the imagery of the lariat: It is only the pull which keeps the rope in action; there is never a disconnection between the ends of the rope. The pull of the upper arm, starting at the shoulder, gauges the level at which tone is produced (key bed, for all practical purposes) and is the arbiter for the actions which connect this pull with the key bed.

Vertical action and horizontal progression (action for finding positions up and down the keyboard) actually are synchronized, but horizontal progression will be described later. Vertical action involves: striking C by the pull of the upper arm (the tip of the elbow moves downward as the upper arm moves back towards the torso) with the forearm, hand, and fingers in a fixed position.

This position, to allow the greatest arc of distance between a low wrist and a high wrist, will be with the low wrist — extension of the forearm and extension of the hand. The pull of the upper arm brings the thumb in contact with the resistance of the key bed.

D, E, F, and G are produced as the low wrist changes to high wrist. Now, the pull involves a turning of the humerus, and this turning lifts the tip of the elbow away from the torso as the hand begins its flexion which produces part of the down-action for control of the key-drop.

But, just as the loop of the lariat never stops turning because it is controlled by the pull of the arm, which also never ceases its turnings, the pull for D, E, F, and G is involved with the taking of the key-drop by a lifting of the upper arm which tips the hand down. Take an exaggerated turn which lifts the elbow as high as possible while still maintaining contact with the key bed, in order to sense the relationship of the upper-arm pull to hand flexion. Hand flexion is a positive down-action for taking vertical distance of the key-drop. Then, at the last possible fraction of a second, the finger becomes alerted (positive in its action) for receiving the power for tone. The finger connects with the key bed by vitalizing its stance, rather than by an action which is positive in the intention of striking the key (taking the vertical distance). The above sentence is good imagery for describing finger action, for it will result in a greater use of the upper-arm action and hand flexion. Anything which will produce a greater control with the upper arm furthers continuity in action and a rhythm.

The down-action, necessary for tone production, involves the upper-arm pull, flexion of the hand, and, at the very last second before the tone is produced, a flexion of the finger.

The in-between-tones action deals with the change in relation between the upper arm, forearm, and hand.

The speed with which the key is lowered — the speed of the delivery of the power for tone — will determine the loudness of the tone. In a slow tempo the relationship of the action of the upper arm, forearm, and hand must be such that the sensation of going forward to the close of the musical statement (ripping the five tones C, D, E, G, F) is not interrupted. The time unit for the delivery of power is minute in comparison with the actual time between the striking of tones.

The delivery of power has the same characteristics as the slow-motion picture we observe: The flowing action is not interfered with, so far as the eye can see. We feel no stop in the flow of procedure toward the musical goal *if* the delivery of power is accurate — accurate in the sense that is it not anticipated nor prolonged, but simply used for the one split second when it is productive of tone, when the total machinery arrives at the level where tone is produced, the key bed.

There is no better means for sensing this relationship of action between tones and the action for tone production then playing staccato in a very slow tempo, but this must be a staccato which does not alter any procedure by the upper arm, forearm, or hand. The staccato must simply permit the finger to become less active at the hand-knuckle immediately after the current of power for tone has been created. Taking infinite pains to perfect both the sensation and the relationship will help to produce the extreme subtlety in nuances of time and dynamics which is essential for a musical statement of great beauty. The staccato also creates the alertness which is a necessary factor for speed and, thus, helps to prevent action in a slow tempo from becoming sluggish and inept (this is very important). If the word *staccato* produces an automatic up-action in the forearm or hand all these relationships will change, and the desired results for continuity between tones will not develop.

Random Notes

The physical counterpart of playing toward a down beat or playing off of an up beat: Playing toward the down beat is like the action of a grace note toward the principal tone. Playing off of an up beat is like playing five tones and holding the stance taken for the first tone.

* * *

Fulcrum — the word is meaningful and accurate, but at no time can we use a word which is more commonly associated with machinery and have it fully illustrate what happens in the human machinery. The fulcrums in the body are alive and responsive — they are never solid or rigid. Rather, they are a pliant, alive, resistant force, and this resistant force is always an integral part of the rhythmic flow. For instance, the upper arm is the fulcrum for the forearm, but use a fling of the forearm — a quick extension — and one easily sees that the upper arm moves forward; or flex the forearm quickly, and the upper arm moves backward. Both of these movements of the upper arm are a part of the mechanism of forearm movement: The alternating action between the forearm and the hand always involves the upper arm.

The action of the upper arm, in relation to the mechanics of the forearm, is no less important for being involuntary. If the upper arm moves in and out, it adjusts to the keyboard and, actually, it is this give-and-take in the action between the two large levers which allows the consistent control of the pull in the upper arm (like the lariat) to operate without ever disconnecting the hand from the keyboard.

Watch the point of the elbow when the pull of the upper arm is operating in any brilliant passage; it is always in motion. The feeling — the awareness of the positive action of the upper arm — is that of guiding the hand into position as well as furnishing power for tone, while maintaining control of key level. But the positive controls do not balk the movement which is so definitely a part of the forearm action. There is no such thing in the entire mechanism as a rigid, set position.

Action, movement, at the periphery is wider and therefore more easily noted by the audience. As a result, attention has become riveted on the hand and fingers. In the great performers (whether they are aware of this or not) all these movements are part and parcel of the central control, and this control always runs the show.

The action of the upper arm as fulcrum helps to solve this problem. Without movement in this fulcrum, activity of the upper arm, the rhythm and the emotional response in the torso could not find their way into tone production. The upper-arm fulcrum has two attributes: constant resistance to the forearm action and constant shifting in position (movement in all directions), as the forearm functions for its contribution to the coverage of distance and the use of power for tone.

The torso is the fulcrum for the arm — the playing mechanism as well as the source of the emotional response to the music. The torso is the great reservoir of power, and it is of the utmost importance that it function as the fulcrum for all activity of the arm, with complete unity and blending of activity between them, even though the torso is the stable part of the mechanism. It is the fulcrum which is grounded, as it were; but never let that mean that the torso becomes a block of sheer weight which feels both stodgy and stolid. The torso, when well used, sits and feels like a buoyant dancer who responds vividly to the creative quality of the music, for the torso does indeed express the varied moods of the music which is being performed.

This expression of the emotional response to the music is the very source of the rhythm which brings to life all the beauty inherent in the music. Its relation to the upper-arm control of distance and power is one of association through its functioning as a fulcrum. Its relation to the expression of emotion is that of a creative, initiating action. It must act, and it must be *permitted* to act because emotion *must* be expressed. Again we see that the fulcrum-activity does not inhibit a positive and creative action, such as the expression of emotion in response to the mood of the music.

Nothing is more damaging to a simple and expressive statement of the music than the well-established belief that a superior technical equipment is the result of training all levers for independence in action. There is never independence in the sense that one lever produces the power for tone independently of other levers. The action, movement, in the fulcrums proves this.

Even independence between the arms is a false concept. Both arms are dependent upon the torso for its acting as a fulcrum and for its emotional response to the music. If one arm picks up preponderantly the emotional quality of the torso, there will result an inadequate performance which lacks subtlety in expressing the mood of the music. Even rests should be played by both arms consistently; there should never be relaxation during rests, a letting-down or letting-go of the musical mood. Quite the reverse: Both arms are always alive and subject to the same emotional current from the torso. When this is not the case, and one arm rests in between activity for tone production (in other words, does not stay active in between articulations and during rests), there is never the same kind of control in dynamics which is produced when there is constant tapping of the emotional current of the torso by both arms. The proof of this statement can only be made by contrasting a phrase produced with an emotional rhythm, channeled by both arms, and a phrase with expression only in one arm.

*   *
  *

Does mechanical practice ever *sound* like an emotional performance? Since it is the emotional performance that is the *only* desired result of all contact with music, the sooner practice involves the necessary attributes of the real performance, the sooner we shall have more beautiful performances to listen to.

*   *
  *

Teaching should be geared to finding ways and means of making sure that the emotional reaction to the music does involve a musical statement — a completed idea. Practice must not become involved with stressing separate tones, or even separating tones. This is a challenge, but it must be met. It is not safe to trust to luck when the greater the talent the greater the sensitivity to pitch. This sensitivity to pitch also produces a tendency to be involved with each separate tone as an entity in itself and, thus, tends to produce a note-by-note performance.

If, at the beginning, learning has always involved the rhythm of the idea, the desired blending of activities has a good chance. But, if details are stressed at the beginning, there are innumerable chances for going wrong in the process of developing the entire mechanism as a unified whole.

It is the rhythm of form, the movements related to the complete statement, which must channel the emotional expression welling up in the torso. How can this channeling be taught? All answers to these problems can be found in the music itself, if a basic rhythm has been established. This problem of channeling emotion involves the selection of tones which should become one continuous strand — the strand of the emotional rhythm. These tones can always be found because the composer created the form with them.

The thing to remember is that the performer must have physical actions which weave these related tones into one strand. There must be a continuous action which lasts as long as the musical form which is being performed. Then, and only then, can the details of musical speech be made to enhance, and not clutter, the production of musical form. The strand must be sufficiently strong *emotionally*, so that it won't be broken by the accumulation of details which are part of its beauty but not the strong thread of progression. For example: Play a waltz with the emotional response primarily attached to the melodic line, and there will be no waltz which will captivate the audience. A waltz is a dance first of all. Play the fundamental basses with the lilt and grace one sees and feels when watching a great dancer or skater, and the melody will be more beautiful and graceful, and the delight of the audience will be instant in its response.

*   *   *

The performer's emotional attachment to the physical actions he uses for performance can give him great satisfaction and still be all wrong for projecting a musical idea. For example, a waltz will not have its dancing lilt if the performer is not as involved with his left hand as he is with the right. The *Gibet* of Ravel also illustrates this point. This is a gruesome picture of a dead man swinging from a gallows. The piece will be totally ineffective if the performer is involved emotionally only with the melody line; but, if the insistent repeated notes are played as inevitably as doom itself, then an emotional picture can be projected which makes a tremendous impact. The melody is not less effective because of this insistence of the repeated tones; quite the reverse, it becomes increasingly poignant.

One could go on *ad infinitum*, for every composition needs this selective quality in determining the projection of its inherent emotional quality. Is it reasonable to believe that teaching does not need to be concerned with the physical action which produces this selective quality?

If faulty habits have been established, it is imperative that new, right habits take their place. This is the teacher's great opportunity for helping talented pianists who are bogged down because of overstressing details.

* * *

The torso acts as a fulcrum and is always part of the action of the upper arm.

* * *

The ripped chord of five tones (C,D,E,F,G) illustrates these vital factors: (1) Power of the arm is used at the bottom of the key. (2) Only the action of the powerful lever is felt when the chord is ripped with speed and brilliance.

It should be the aim of the teacher to make this action of the upper arm so vivid that it can absorb all the actions of the other levers and, by so doing, dampen the eagerness of the too-active fingers both to find the tones and to strike them ahead of the upper arm.

* * *

In the Etude, Op. 25, No. 12, the action of the wrist must be such that it allows the power of the upper arm to throw the hand into action (from octave to octave) — the upper arm plus the forearm of course.

* * *

The two arms should always feel as one, not two separate entities, and should always maintain a relationship with the torso. There must be only one stem and source for all activity if it is to be simple.

* * *

Playing off of an impulse means that the upper arm absorbs action of the smaller levers.

*   *   *

To learn spacing use patterns. The lack of tonal sensuousness in the scale-structure of the pattern enables the student to take the ear away from the pitch-pattern and concentrate on the sensing of the physical action.

*   *   *

The body assists in the action, but it does not initiate the action for distance. All distance, as well as the basic rhythm of form, is initiated with the upper arm.

*   *   *

The playing mechanism is the whole arm backed up by the torso.

*   *   *

Power must be so snug that it chokes out the fingers.

*   *   *

Check constantly for preparation by the hand or fingers. Constantly use a transfer of sensation to get the power of the upper arm to be tone-producing.

*   *   *

The torso should favor the difficult distance. Be sure the torso is alert before starting.

*   *   *

Arpeggios use the kind of action one uses in twirling a lariat.

*   *   *

In slowing down the ripped chord, keep the action of the upper arm dominant. Do not emphasize the movements of articulation. Do not come up!*

*   *   *

* See "kick-off" in Glossary.

Passing the fifth finger over the thumb, the hand carries the fingers almost relaxed. The action at the wrist is one of delivering power which originates further back (torso, upper arm, forearm), not one of intention of controlling distance. The trill involves the same kind of freedom at the wrist; action must come through the wrist from further back.

*   *   *

After working on a detail, always return to the kind of practice which will absorb the detail into the large form.

*   *   *

Faulty coordination always involves overactivity in articulation.

*   *   *

Never be satisfied with a feeling that there are too many tones for comfort. Use an outline until the basic rhythm forces the less important tones into the groove of a long-line progression.

*   *   *

For all speed and brilliant passage work, the action at the wrist is one which is propelled by the upper arm and forearm.

*   *   *

Whenever there is exaggeration in action by a short lever, play the passage in parallel motion; it will take the exaggeration out, and the playing will favor the similar action of the upper arms.

*   *   *

Make continuity in the action for arriving so important that it will carry emotion with it (will make the rhythm the emotional outlet).

*   *   *

Avoid legato in passing.

*   *   *

Never use consecutive keys to solve a problem in passing. (Eds. This means don't use C,D,E, and F,G,A, but, instead, use C,D,E, and an octave higher C,D,E.) Use wide spaces. This gives an opportunity for action by the upper arm between tones.

*   *   *

No matter what point attention has been focused upon, the most important point to take care of is the basic rhythm. You begin and end with that.

*   *   *

Get ready to suspend. Do not get ready to hit. In a fresh practicing session take time to sense the two arms as a unit and to make the torso active. Don't start staccato, start legato with a musical idea and run into staccato.

*   *   *

Rhythm, Not Editor's Marks

❧≽❧

Every thoughtful person is aware of the difference in interpretation of two great artists in playing the same composition. We cannot plumb the creative perception of the artist, but we should be able to approach a clear understanding of the tools he uses for projecting his art.

At the outset, we must admit that the differences in interpretation cannot be explained by the differences in editions. Even though every mark of editing was put there by the composer himself, and the musicians do respect a composer's marks, the interpretations still vary.

What we, as an audience, hear is a variation in the use of the two great factors through which interpretation is expressed: dynamics and nuances of time.

Because the piano tone starts diminishing in intensity the moment it is sounded, the holding of the tone is not the channel for the expression of emotion, as it is with the instruments where the intensity is controlled by the holding of the tone. Thus, the pianist is practically without the holding process for the expression of his emotion, so far as the audience is concerned. But what the artist does in between striking keys will very definitely influence the succeeding tones in dynamics and timing.

For the artist to be able to control the quality of the tone he produces, he must be in contact with the vibrator which creates the tone. Therefore, the pianist cannot "color" his tone. The felt hammer, which contacts the string, can only be made to vary its intensity in hitting. So, what the artist does with nuances of time and dynamics creates the variations in interpretation which the audience hears.

On the printed page there are indications of rhythm of meter, note values, a few remarks, necessarily vague, dealing with mood, tempo, and marks of intensity for delivery of power.   But every sensitive performer knows that two accents are rarely played the same way, although they look exactly alike.   There must be a factor somewhere which is not present on the printed page and cannot be indicated; but, it is the factor responsible for the variation produced, which we, the audience, so clearly hear in the two performances.

That factor, I feel sure, is the rhythm of form — the rhythm of the musical idea.

This rhythm must hold sway somewhere in the artist's being, consciously or unconsciously, and provides for him the channel for his emotional expression.   It helps him to make the details beautiful and, at the same time, have them contribute their beauty to the large, musical statement, instead of attracting attention simply to a detail. It is this fitting of details into a larger mold which creates the essential difference in two performances; and there can be no fitting-in of details if there is not a larger form into which they can be fitted.

An intellectual concept of the large form and its details is never sufficient to create the actual subtlety in nuance which the greatest beauty in performance demands. There must be a physical action which feels that large form, which actually creates it.   Ignoring in our teaching this physical action which produces the great rhythm of form and stressing the actions which produce only the details is largely responsible for playing which has all-too-little relation to the beauty produced by the artist.

Paradoxically, it is the ear which is, no doubt, the offender in producing both the teaching and the learning which ignore the great rhythm of form.   The pitch of successive tones is part of the very essence of music. But these successive pitches were never set down by the composer except to fulfill a musical statement, and that musical statement most certainly involved a rhythm. The greater the artist the more sensitive are all his perceptions, and the great performers have kept the relationship between the commanding rhythm and the satisfying of the pitch perceptions. They have kept this relationship with no assistance from teaching but practically in spite of teaching; for teaching, so far as one can learn, has always stressed the physical action only in relation to the production of details. But, the physical production of details is not identical with the physical production of the basic rhythm of form, which underlies all the notes of a musical composition. A natural coordination would have a chance to assist in the production of details if the larger motivation came first. With details first and always stressed, there are innumerable pitfalls for any complete use or understanding of a rhythm of form, and, certainly, every block which could prevent nature's coordination is present, although nature's coordination is the only one which will provide the subtle balance in activity necessary for creating great beauty. Trust the printed page for pitch, but trust only a surging rhythm for the emotional expression which can govern rhythmic nuance and dynamics.

It is amazing to discover how different is the relation of editor's marks to playing when the playing is driven by a strong, basic rhythm, from the relation between the two when the playing is basically in response to the details on the page and a concept based on intellectual analysis. The printed page is almost crude in what it suggests, in comparison with the subtleties which a sensitive rhythm will create.

Practicing a Performance

✻

If one considers the elements of a creative performance and contrasts them with the elements which usually constitute what is called "practice," with its preponderance of working over details, it becomes immediately apparent that "practice" develops none of the habits requisite for a performance.

Elements of Performance:

(1) Physical action which produces the rhythm of form. This involves continuity in tone-producing power toward the destination of a completed musical statement.

(2) Heightened emotion, a reaction to the beauty of the music, which changes the entire muscular coordination and the quality of the performer's involvement.

(3) A projection of the musical message.

Practice Which Denies the Above Attributes:

(1) Repetition of a detail with emphasis on accuracy.

(2) Usually includes a slow tempo with an attendant exaggeration of detailed articulation, without any relation to making music.

(3) Never uses continuity of action in the upper arm, where the basic rhythm is implemented, but uses movements of articulation — almost exclusively finger action.

(4) Practices a note-wise procedure, because each tone is produced with a separate initiation of power. No music making is helped by this habit — quite the reverse.

(5) Develops independent, unrelated activity of the short levers, uncoordinated by a basic rhythm.

This serves to exaggerate the opposition in movements between the two hands and forearms which occurs in parallel scale passages: The untwist of one forearm accompanies the twist of the other in rotary action, strong fingers of one hand are used with weak fingers of the other Also, movements of articulation are exaggerated and made more important, instead of developing the continuous movement of the upper arm which is the *central* power and hence the only power that can automatically coordinate all the actions of the entire arm.

But virtuosity — speed and brilliance — is the result of the two arms working as a *unit*, the same kind of balanced activity in both, using their common fulcrum — the torso. What is needed is not opposition, which exaggerates movements of articulation, but a balanced action, which emphasizes the equality and ease of action in the two upper arms, with a flow of energy and activity between the two as a part of continuity toward a destination.

All repetition should be done for the sake of producing skill for a complete musical performance. Obviously, repetition develops habits of action. How can one argue that developing habits not conducive to performance is a profitable expenditure of time and energy? There is no validity in producing habits which are extraneous, and even contrary, to the habits needed for a performance.

If repetition is to result in a beautiful performance, it must use the elements of such a performance and not elements which impede it.

The elements of momentum can be clearly recognized when speed and wide distance on the keyboard are in use, for instance in M. Rosenthal's *Papillons*. This momentum is born of activity in the upper arm, and this activity should be ceaseless and tone producing for every tone, with a strong aim at the destination point, such as in the glissando — the completely simple example. Thus, this momentum is a part of tone production. In a slow movement the change is like the change in a movie from normal speed to slow motion.

Pull is the action which flexes the forearm, as when a boy shows his muscle. The sensation of flexion is so strongly that of a pull that it confused me for a long time into thinking the sensation of pull was in the action of the upper arm. Actually, the upper arm does pull toward the torso when it takes the key-drop, as frequently happens, but the upper arm continues in propelling its power into key in any direction that becomes useful as it utilizes the time element between tones, no matter whether a fast momentum or a slow-motion progression is operating.*

The real point is that the upper arm, both upper arms, must *create* and maintain the rhythm of the musical idea, no matter what goes on in the matter of articulation of varying patterns. Thus, there should be greater involvement in the *unification* of the power of the upper arms (for example, in the Chopin Etude, Op. 10, No. 12) for the creation of the emotional rhythm of the soprano part, than concentration on the entirely *different* patterns of soprano and bass. For that reason practice which separates the soprano from bass and creates habits of feeling differences rather than unification is a hindrance rather than a help.

In reading Curt Sachs' *Rhythm and Tempo*, not once did I find dynamics mentioned as a fundamental instigator of a basic rhythm. Nor, if I recall accurately, does he distinguish between the physical actions which deal with a basic rhythm and with articulation. What I have in mind is that there is no indication that two

* See Foreword, p. 13.

kinds of physical action are involved in playing: One (the basic, underlying, slow rhythm) has continuity for unifying tones into a phrase; the second action or, rather, set of actions is one which deals with articulations (provides for power contacting key for tone). These are separate actions which dovetail into the larger, continuous action of power.

An illustration of just how faulty ideas can be, and how possible it is for them to catch on, is the Virgil Clavier — the silent keyboard for going through finger gymnastics. It refutes every sound principle of the process by which the body operates at its maximum efficiency — is fully coordinated for production. Yet it had a vogue and was used quite extensively at one time, because the traditional concept stressed that fingers must be trained for independence.

The problem of activity in the upper arm (both for power in producing tones and continuity in activity between tones) as it heads for the musical destination is one which needs to be dealt with in a very detailed manner.

Beware forever of the held tone! If it is held with static power there will, of necessity, be a fresh use of power for the next tone and, thereby, a frustration of the greatest subtlety in modeling the phrase. *Static holding means static listening, and a performance of the utmost sensitivity cannot take place under those circumstances.*

Teaching must be concerned primarily with implementing a continuity in power (activity in the upper arms) which is active from the first tone through every tone until the musical message has been projected. Rests, as well as tones, must be filled with activity.

Independence of action, whether with fingers, hands, or arms, forms habits that are counter to all simplicity and ease in playing. Cooperation, *unification* is the thing to be stressed and developed as the basis for a virtuoso technique and subtlety in projecting musical ideas.

The use of a basic rhythm — the physical activity which produces it — as the channel for the emotional output (instead of actions of articulation) is akin to a distilling process for the musical message. Only the purest statement comes forth.

What is meant by "playing off of a tone" and "playing toward the important tone"?

There will be no lilt and grace to the music unless one understands clearly the difference between the two in stating a phrase. The music was not written to be played either this way, or that way; it was very definitely intended to be played in only one manner. And there is always a very definite, though very fine, distinction in the physical counterpart of the manner of playing to be chosen. It is *imperative* that the physical action be right for the right lilt.

If one is a teacher it is imperative that one understand these physical subtleties in activity. I do not mean that power can be weighed, analyzed, and prescribed exactly. This cannot be done, because muscles which create this power act in areas, and, so far, no live pianist has ever been dissected while performing. So we do not know the exact quantity of energy that is delivered by any given muscle.

But, there is a relationship between the activity of the upper arm and the actions of the front levers — forearm, hand, and fingers — which extend this activity. This relationship can be clearly understood as it functions to create beautifully distilled musical ideas. What's more, it *must* be understood. In any case, this distillation is always a part of the kind of projection of musical ideas which is present in a great performance.

For the creation of a basic rhythm, as well as the conservation of energy, there must be perfect timing for the delivery of energy for producing tone; this delivery must be aimed for that *precise level* in the key-drop where the hammer is tripped and hits the string. One reaches this level ahead of resistance — the key bed, but it so close to key-bed resistance that one can only sense it as a sure aim at that level — never, never below that level. Unnecessarily long and hard sticking to the key bed, using more energy than is needed, is the inevitable result of aiming too low (in a sense, *below* the key bed).

Any holding of the power in a static fashion for the production of one tone cuts down the time unit between tones which should be used for going forward. Unless the time unit between tones is used to the fullest extent possible for that purpose, there is a disruption of the going-forward action by the upper-arm power, and that action is an essential way of implementing the basic rhythm.

Perfect timing: The precise delivery of power at tone-producing level, never holding that power jammed against the key bed even a fraction of a second after tone has been produced, is part of the process which one can call "focusing." It is focusing energy for tone that produces the clarity and clean playing of the master of his instrument.

Energy for tone, the action which responds to the aural image, always is the responsibility of the upper arms — action at the center of the radius of activity of the playing mechanism. Continuity in rhythm never means continuity with only one arm. When the two arms are in complete balance, activity passes back and forth between the two with no interruption in the flow of activity forward. The upper arms bring the hands in contact with tone — at least they should. This means that the upper arms gauge the distance for level — *control* the level at which the energy for tone is released. Since the upper arms do not touch the keys, but their action is extended by the forearms, hands, and fingers, there is no chance for the upper arms to be effective in tone production unless the timing of the action of the levers which extend the primary actions of the upper arms is unified, not separated from the upper arms.

* * *

A change in patterns in the midst of a composition tends to change the balance in activity between articulation and the basic rhythmic power. Consciously trying to maintain the same balance of activity when such a transition occurs will help to keep the performance both simple and graceful.

*   *   *

Placing the hands on the keyboard and striking the initial tone of a composition should be done in such a way that the upper arm takes charge of depressing the key. The upper arm has only one direction of action akin to the vertical drop of the key. When the pianist is ready to play, his stance is one in which the elbow does not hang but is slightly in front of the torso. Therefore, if the lever, of which the elbow is the end, does control the key-drop, it moves away from the keyboard and toward the torso; that is why it is completely right to describe this as a pull.

Now it is obvious that the upper arm cannot keep on pulling toward the body. In order to have that pull available — that is, to have the power of the upper arm available at all times for taking the key-drop for important tones — there must, of necessity, be an action for having the top of the elbow rise (as against lowering when it takes the key-drop) so that it can take the key-drop when the pianist desires to produce an important tone primarily with the entire arm. To find out what happens when the elbow rises (this rise may be no more than the distance of the key-drop, or it may be considerably larger) will provide the solution to what the forearm, hand, and fingers do. The manner of usage is always determined by the pattern of the music: whether there are wide skips or a close pattern of consecutive keys, whether the tempo is slow or fast, whether the tonal pattern uses black and white keys, or only black, or only white. The rise of the upper arm may well be exaggerated to carry emotional output and projection. I find it the surest cure for excessive activity in the hand and fingers.

*   *   *

Projection of emotion in performance is only achieved with a physical intensity that involves the entire body. One fairly leaps into a rhythmic propulsion which makes the music come to life.

*   *   *

The exaggerated rise of the upper arm for the purpose of expressing emotion and stimulating a rhythmic activity between tones poses a problem when subtlety in timing a slow, lyric statement is desired, and when great speed is needed. Then, it is necessary to express the emotional intensity by a balanced, suspended power with a minimum of activity for tone production — a holding action which accepts the tones which are essential to the musical statement, instead of taking the key-drop entirely with the full-arm stroke. When speed is needed, one uses as many tones under one application of power as can be produced in one stance; the power moves horizontally into another position on the keyboard only when it is necessary, and not before.

*   *   *

People usually do not work hard enough when they practice; they are not completely involved both physically, mentally, and emotionally. In short, they are not practicing a performance, but doing something limited like learning the notes, etc. Of course, practicing a complete performance is the only way to practice.

*   *   *

In the midst of a lesson I suddenly learned how to teach the trill in double thirds (the opening of Chopin Etude, Op. 25, No. 6). I had never been satisfied with previous results. This day, after the pupil played a little Schubert Waltz, I asked her to improvise something in three-quarter time and to use four fingers of the right hand in a repeated action, then to open the four fingers into a double-note trill. Afterwards, we started to improvise again in the same meter and, without interruption, shifted to *alla breve* and, thus, to the opening of the Etude, and this worked. This emphasizes that mastering a difficult pattern is best done by doing something quite different from the actual pattern which produces the difficulty. One must first find some pattern which permits a rhythm to have its way easily; after that, one attempts to transfer the sensation of an easy, lilting rhythm into the pattern one is trying to solve.

*   *   *

Readiness for power delivery, not relaxation, is a requisite for speed and brilliance. If the hand is alert — has a sense of chord formation, which involves what I call having all the fingers feel equal in length — and if the hand feels close or snug to the shoulder, which again means no relaxation at either the wrist or the elbow but, on the contrary, a readiness to be used, and, finally, if there is an active power in the upper arm that is forever the response to the aural image, then the performer will have a chance to tap his actual capacity for beauty, speed, and brilliance.

*   *   *

Using M. Rosenthal's *Papillons* one can make vivid the realization that the rhythm produced by the arms united with the torso, is always tone-producing as it travels from highlight to highlight. The movement of the power lever (upper arm) is always a part of tone production; think it the entire power and there is more truth than in thinking of the power delivered by other levers. Shorter levers meet the power of the upper arm and supplement it, as the upper arm gauges distance and level; these shorter levers, when tucking in tones, must *never* take the key-drop ahead of the power lever. All too often the basic rhythm is a feeling of continuity from important tone to important tone; that is not enough. That continuity in action must also be tone producing

— sharing in the power used for producing the tucked-in tones.

In line with the previous statement, there cannot be too much emphasis on the activity of the upper shaft as it skates its way into the key-drop and the resulting tone, and goes on to the next one, always maintaining its sense of closeness to tone (control of the key level at which the hammer trips to produce tone).

* * *

The shortest application of power is always made on-the-wing, as it were, when the upper arm is actively on its way.

* * *

Ripping five consecutive tones is an excellent example of a *minimum* of articulation by fingers. Such an adjustment of the upper-arm activity is right for all tonal patterns, but the balance between upper-arm activity (or control) and the amount of necessary articulation closer to the keyboard may vary with different musical patterns when top speed is involved.

* * *

How big a tonal pattern can be taken with one upper-arm impulse? As long as power covers the five fingers it can be fairly quiet. It must be active with a shift of direction — in and out. (Op. 25, No. 2.)

* * *

The torso is the fulcrum for both arms. Only when it is subtly balanced, can a rhythm be a penetrating factor. If one arm is not actively involved and balanced while the other arm plays, there can't be a balanced torso.

* * *

A great help in getting a basic rhythm is to play a

pianissimo staccato, with the upper arm controlling key level (delivering power at level).

*   *   *

Dynamics do not necessarily involve a rhythm, but rhythm will involve dynamics.

*   *   *

Myths About the Piano
and Pianists

What is a harsh tone? What is a hard or disagreeable tone? What is meant when someone says, "He played with a singing tone"? Is it certain that there is a "beautiful legato" in a beautiful performance? What does produce speed and brilliance? Is it strong fingers and wrists "like steel"?

A pianist, as a listener, is, of necessity, conditioned by his practicing habits. The above phrases reflect a way of listening which is induced by the practicing habits, by the particular means used to produce beauty. But suppose these habits, these means are faulty? Why, then no beautiful performance will result, no matter how much talent is present. Nothing but a basic rhythm can make all the details fit into a musical statement so that there can be room for all the tones, dignity, subtlety, and an emotional intensity which simply commands a rapt attention from the audience.

Following unreal, mythical goals in one's practice will not produce good and real results except occasionally, in spite of the goals. Not even the presence of considerable talent assures a successful result with faulty practice. It is essential that we face up to what is possible or attainable in the realm of piano playing, and what is not.

Here are a few common phrases, used constantly by pianists and listeners in general, which quite obviously have no valid relation to piano playing: color, a singing tone, marvelous legato, beautiful tone, harsh tone, rich tone, brittle tone, strong fingers, strong wrists. How completely misleading to describe piano playing with the same terms that are used for the violin or the voice. Actually, these are blocks to learning to play well and to hear accurately and sensitively. No performer can color tone unless he is in contact with the vibrator which produces tone. How can a tone be a singing one, when it starts diminishing the moment it is produced? How can a tone be harsh, when all that can happen to it is an increase in volume? Of course the piano is a percussive instrument, but the noises of percussion are not the tone of pitch. Brittle tone — well, does anyone really know what is meant? Marvelous fingers! Every pianist who has labored at finger exercises will give credit to fingers. Nonetheless, the reality is that when speed and brilliance are involved all the talented people do the same thing: use their powerful muscles governing the upper arm against the bony structure of the fingers.

If there were an easy way of establishing productive habits, after destructive habits have been firmly learned, the life of a teacher would be considerably less arduous. For example, take listening. If a player has the habit of using a separate initiation of power for each tone, as is the case when "independent" fingers produce the power for tone, then that player will listen to each tone in turn and not to the phrase as a whole. And simply no one will be able to persuade him that his listening helps to defeat his desire for an exciting performance.

There is a vast difference between good imagery in talking about performance and inaccuracy in the use of words which describe attributes which simply are not pertinent to the piano and which masquerade as imagery. Using words which have no validity in regard to the piano reflects listening habits that are conditioned by faulty playing habits — usually the products of a playing mechanism conditioned to a notewise procedure in the use of power.   Practicing to make the fingers "independent" and listening conditioned by such practice cause the pianist always to be aware of individual notes and never of the phrase-by-phrase form.   Such listening blocks hearing what actually does take place.

One cannot "color" a piano tone, but the word is habitually used to describe a sensitive performance.   There is no such thing as a "singing" tone with the piano.   The piano tone diminishes in volume from its very inception. What is meant is a succession of tones which leads the ear forward to a completed statement because of the subtlety in the use of dynamics.   There is no "harsh" tone.   There is simply a succession of loud tones which have no subtlety in gradation of intensity and perhaps, in fact very likely, have a greater amount of percussive noise than is necessary, because of a faulty delivery of power — power delivered below the level where the hammer trips as the key is depressed.   It is only fair to state that these percussive noises do not carry in the hall and cannot be heard beyond the first few rows; of course the lack of sensitivity in gradation of dynamics is heard.

This list of inaccuracies is only a small sample of meaningless words (meaningless in relation to the piano) which are constantly used in reference to playing the piano.

Splashing[*]

All my life I have remembered the virtuosity and abandon of my performances on the window sill before there was a piano in the house. Because I have been teaching most of my life and struggling to find the answers to achieving an exciting performance, I have thought, "If only there were a way to capture and preserve that childlike abandon and delight in performance while an equipment for playing is in progress. What a tremendous step ahead we should be in achieving our goals!"

Now I think I have a flash of insight as to how that might be achieved. I had an excellent opportunity to experiment while teaching an adult who wants to play the piano. He plays the viola. He literally has no time to practice, but he is a gifted person — a cultivated musician with a flair for projecting a musical idea.

Knowing that the prime requisite for a beautiful performance is the aural image translated into tone by using a basic rhythm for the emotional outlet, I decided we would achieve a glorious and spectacular emotional rhythm first, even if everything else had to be ignored temporarily.

This is the process to date: We use "chords" or, more accurately, tone clusters; I mean by this that the palm is *never* flabby or even half loose, but always the five

---

[*] This is a rough draft of a new idea A. W. jotted down in November, 1956.

154

fingers are held in readiness to stand up under the arm power. The actual notes of this "chord" don't at all matter. We use any rhythmic pattern, from a piece of music or improvised; the chords are "splashed" all over the keyboard.

For instance, he will play a part of the Two-Part Invention in A minor by J.S. Bach; this means that chords will be crashed all over the keyboard. No attempt at any kind of tonal accuracy is made to avoid any chance of a notewise procedure in the Invention; the one thing one aims for is this violent, flamboyant explosion of chords. After this expression of a desire to possess all the resources of the piano he returns to the Invention with the intention of maintaining the exciting, rhythmic performance so easily attained when accuracy is not demanded. Incidentally, those pieces which he plans to have in his repertoire, are taught to him by rote. Of course he can do his own reading, but that involves a fussing at the keyboard to find the right tone and all "fussing" is out.

Then I will be asked, "What's this?" I will answer, on the basis of what he will have played, "Brahms D minor Concerto," or "Ravel Concerto for the Left Hand" or the name of any other virtuoso piece which he knows but which is completely out of his range for playing. He does know them, the aural image is there, and he dramatizes it with every bit of emotional response to the music that is in his being. No one could possibly miss the intention — the piece is there in all its glory except for the exact tones. You might say, "Then it isn't there at all," but I assure you that the listening is fun because the rhythm is so exciting.

Of course I am dealing, in this case, with an excellent musician and a person who expresses emotion with his body whenever he touches music. But, if we can find a wedge into this area of expressing emotion with the basic rhythm, we can, by degrees, learn how to make it applicable to all students.

Adaptation is never as difficult as finding a *clue* to a

realistic approach to a problem. This problem of dramatizing a musical idea can't wait until there is a playing mechanism which can take care of distance, speed, and accuracy. The learning process will be most efficient when we start out by using this most important factor before there is any reasonable chance of using it with tonal accuracy in any given piece.

All teachers should be concerned with learning how to use an exciting rhythm at the beginning — not after every other habit has been formed that could make it difficult to use a rhythm. Splashing chords with abandon all over the keyboard in an improvisational manner, using rhythmic patterns and getting closer and closer to the related keyboard positions, when imitating a bravura piece, seems to be a real clue to the problem.

Successful Piano Teaching*

Playing the piano is like skating or riding a bicycle. It is a physical process involving natural ease, efficiency, and complete coordination. This may sound terribly obvious, but many pianists and piano teachers do not seem to understand this simple fact and its implications. The player is told often enough that listening to oneself is the important thing in practice and performance. But he should be told more often that the physical action of the performer conditions his listening. Unless these two processes, physical activity and listening, are fully coordinated, the pupil will never achieve ease, enduring technical facility, and complete enjoyment of the piano.

The music student should begin by playing by ear. He must learn to read, quite obviously, but he should be an aural learner rather than a visual learner. Observe the ease and accuracy of pupils who have learned to play by ear. Their skill is never attained by those who learned the notes first and then built up a coordination that is dependent on the eye. Notes, after all, are merely symbols for sounds. The pupil who has learned music by the way it sounds hears the tone when he looks at the symbol. The movements that make this imagined tone audible are directed by his ear. They are as fluid, as efficient, as coordinated as his movements when playing without notes.

* An article which appeared in the Dec. 15, 1951 issue of *Musical America*. This version was based on an interview with Abby Whiteside by Robert Sabin. Reprinted by permission of the publisher.

We must not allow separate physical movements or intellectual processes to interfere with this complete coordination. Many pupils listen notewise, because the separate initiation of power involved in the movement of each finger absorbs their attention and prevents them from playing a smooth phrase and from feeling the overall rhythm of the music. Ironically enough, those gifted with absolute pitch have more difficulty with this problem than those with a faulty sense of pitch. They listen so hard to pitch that their bodies overplay in response, and they are likely to pay too much attention to individual tones at the expense of the phrase.

There are two rhythms in music, and the pupil should be helped from the beginning to understand both of them. There is the rhythm of note-values, and there is the rhythm of form. The rhythm of form arises from the work as a whole — the continuous evolution of its pattern and significance, the legato feeling of phrases, and the telling of a coherent musical story. The rhythm of articulation is the rhythm of separate notes; it is a necessary component of playing, but it has no significance unless it is fused into a larger scheme. You cannot play notewise any more than you can speak letterwise. Notes make up a musical speech; it is only when they are combined that they make musical sense. From the beginning, the pupil should think of them as symbols for continuous patterns of sound, not as isolated statements.

The two fundamental factors in acquiring musical skill are the auditory image (what the pupil actually hears in his mind) and the feeling of rhythm. With beginners a long period of rote learning will enable the ears to register tone more easily. Pantomime may be used to enable the body to feel the exhilarating rhythm of the music. When the physical processes are perfectly coordinated and fused with the emotional expression of the music, the teacher will observe the ease and freedom that one finds in the movement of a fine skater or acrobat.

Jazz players are always right if they have not been

taught. They have a tune in their ears and a rhythm in their bodies. They embellish the melody, but they never disturb the rhythm. Their amazing facility is based on the coordination of all the factors of producing music. Nearly all of them play by ear, although they can read notes when they wish to. They choose a tune that has an alluring rhythm and evolve a complex musical setting without ever losing the directness of impulse and physical control with which they began.

The application of this fact to teaching can be illustrated from personal experience. A former pupil of mine, a well-known popular composer and conductor, returns every now and then. He wants to check up on his problem of listening to too many tones, thereby allowing the rhythm of form to become insufficiently compelling to create the proper balance between a fully coordinated body and the aural image. At one of these check-ups I asked him to improvise a mazurka and then read a Chopin Mazurka. He understood that the goal was to carry over into playing from the printed page the physical rhythm inherent in improvisation. His improvised mazurka was completely sensitive, rhythmic, and delightful. His Chopin Mazurka did not have these qualities. Twice he failed to make a successful transition from the improvising to reading. The third time he was successful, and the result was a completely delightful performance of the Chopin Mazurka. Then, looking a bit puzzled, he said: "But you know it went so fast I didn't hear it." In other words, the first two times the printed page caused him to listen for the pitch of each note symbol for tone. His body was forced to attend to the playing of each tone, and the rhythm of the musical idea as a whole was not expressed. The result was an unmusical performance. When the form-rhythm was maintained as it was in the improvisation the music almost seemed to play itself. There were no interruptions, time lags, or any of the other snags that beset the performer who is conditioned to notewise listening.

In an improvisation you have an idea to complete, and you play ahead towards the completion of phrases and of combinations of phrases. In reading someone else's music you tend to concentrate on written notes rather than on complete ideas. The pitch of individual notes becomes so important in the mind that the ear seeks for particular tones. Often the tone that is so emphasized is not the proper one to make the phrase in which it occurs sound sensitive and well balanced. The pupil should be helped to play with physical directness, as direct as a glissando. Continuity in the use of the power that is tone producing, that flows through like a rhythmic current underneath the separate movements, is all-important.

I applied these principles not long ago to an adult beginner, who did not read music. I started her at once on the little Prelude in C minor (sometimes marked, "For the Lute") by Bach. I did not teach her the notes at first. We worked on a simple rhythm at the first lesson, playing the C minor triad on the first and third beats of a three-four meter. I opened the figuration at the top of the keyboard to prepare her ear for the actual shaping of the work. At the end of two lessons we had established the basic rhythm, and she realized how the figurations opened out of this. In a few more lessons she had learned the notes and was able to open up all the chords she was already playing. At the end of one month she could play the Prelude up to tempo.

The pupil's first approach to the keyboard should be a happy experience, and it should deal with music itself — not with verbal concepts. The first sensation he should have is that when he touches the keyboard he brings a familiar melody to life. The teacher should begin with the most beautiful literature available, not with finger exercises or other such material. The pupil must be involved emotionally and intellectually from the first lesson, no matter how simple the beginning. Let me emphasize once again, he must begin with the ear rather than with the hand. When you start with the hand you are trapped. By setting up a finger technique without coordinating the whole mechanism of the body and involving the emotions, the teacher throws a wrench into the musical machine. The human hand is an extremely sensitive mechanism, and once it has acquired independent habits it stubbornly resists change.

The teacher should begin with the physical sensation and build up to the mental concept, but the physical sensation must involve the entire body. If I told you that you had to remove a splinter from my eye immediately to prevent my becoming blind, you would use not merely your hands but your whole body in concentrating on the task. It is this sort of concentration that must be awakened in the musical beginner. The basic reaction to music, to the mood, one might say, takes place in the torso. The center of the body should have the same relation to the hands that the hub has to the spokes of a wheel or the center to the outside markings of a compass. They should move in rhythmic harmony. If the performer projects his emotional responses to the music from the body, with a feeling of suspended energy and rhythmic continuity, his playing will have smoothness and grace.

He should not worry too much about single notes at the beginning. It is the rhythm of form, as I have called it, that is vital. The pupil's first impressions, which are the most lasting, should not be those of struggling movements to hit right keys. He should feel the over-all rhythm of the music in his body and find an emotional outlet in playing it from this center. If he merely forces his hands to hit the proper keys and tries to express his feeling through this type of localized activity he is on the way to becoming a bad pianist.

The piano presents a special difficulty. The performer sits in front of the instrument and produces tone through vertical action, a series of key-hitting strokes. Yet the pianist must strive for the same infinite rhythmic and dynamic variations that the human voice possesses. He must produce tones by a continuous flow of energy rather than by separate initiations of power. Hum a tune and observe the gradation of tone. The intensity changes constantly as the breath varies automatically with the lilt of the tune. The pianist must achieve a continuous flow of tone-producing power that is as fluid and sensitive as the singer's breath. The musical idea must be the stimulus that produces constant variation in tonal intensity; the hands alone will never enable the pianist to do this, no matter how sensitive or expertly trained they are. The bodily coordination needed must proceed from the inside; the activity must begin in the torso and involve the whole body.

Why do so many pianists sound brilliant and interesting with orchestra and then give dull, insipid solo recitals? One important reason is that many of them have acquired bad habits that disappear temporarily when they perform concertos. They cannot resist the rhythm set up by the orchestra, and they are compelled to play the music in a continuous flow. They have physical freedom and excitement, and at the same time a complete realization of rhythmic control. But in recital they allow their hands and their minds to get between themselves and the music; their old habits reassert themselves; their playing becomes fragmentary, tense, and distorted.

Half of the beauty in piano playing is in the spacing of tones. From the beginning the teacher should work for the ultimate sensitivity of phrasing. The best method is to find works in the great musical literature that are sufficiently simple for beginners, pieces that have a pattern that absorbs all of the complications. Working with this rhythm, the teacher can give the pupil a sensation of solving the mechanics of the music as he learns it by ear. The pupil's sense of distance on the keyboard and the amount of energy he uses in covering it are extremely important. He must be shown that nature coordinates from the center out, and that he must not think of distance merely in terms of moving the hand. He must be given a strong feeling of going forward in each piece that he plays. It is no accident that Toscanini conducts in circles, for it is exactly this sense of continuous flow that he is imparting to the orchestra.

Above all, teachers should remember that nature is the prime factor in playing the piano as in every other human activity. They must help nature, not impose intellectual or physical concepts that cannot be understood and motivated from within the body. The technical miracles that the great pianists perform are miracles of nature.

Experiencing Music
With the Piano *

The people who have the most fun making music are the people who play by ear. That does not mean that they cannot read, but that they learn with their ears; and if they do read, the notes are merely symbols for tones. The printed page is sound to them. How else can you know music, except how it sounds? How do you know a Bach Fugue or a Beethoven Symphony? And since these auditory people learn the music by the way it sounds, the movements which make the imaged tone audible are directed by the ear.

Keep your eye on the ball, says the golfer, knowing that in order to hit it squarely the eye must be the determining factor for bringing all the movements to a focus at the exact distance. Keep your ear on the music, should be the slogan for all musicians, for, since tone must be produced, the ear must be the determining factor for bringing all the movements to a focus at the exact instant tone is desired.

Where are the hosts of piano students of yesterday? Are they still making music? If so, find out if it is not the aural group. The visual learners have stopped playing because it was a task to keep in practice instead of a delight to make music. Only one main artery leads directly into the realm of music: the artery where tone

* Reprinted by permission from the Music Teachers' National Association, *Volume of Proceedings for 1938.*

points the way. Every other avenue is a detour if not a dead-end street.

The only safe beginning for a music student is to play by ear. To believe this completely, one need only observe the ease and accuracy of those students who began in that manner. The skill they develop is never duplicated by those who learned the notes first and built up a coordination depending on the eye. The amazing facility found in all jazz orchestras is good evidence of what goes into the coordination for making music. Practically all of those players can and do play by ear even though they read notes. How did they start? By playing a tune that had an alluring rhythm! Why did they start? Because they wanted to play that tune.

The first trial with music at the keyboard should be a happy experience and, by all rules and regulations of modern education, should deal with music itself and not an approach to it. That can happen if the only reason for touching the keyboard is to bring to life a familiar melody. How can it happen if there are notes to be learned and keys to be named and fingering to be attended to? That process is too difficult to be enjoyed. Doubtless a large part of the reason it endures is that we live in a world in which the eye is accustomed to taking responsibility and it learns more readily than the ear with a large percentage of people. Therefore playing a short piece from the music is a possible tangible result at an early stage, and both teachers and parents want something to show for the time and money spent.

The ideal setup for giving students the opportunity to learn to play the piano by ear would be to have small groups working together daily. Instead, too often there is a half-hour private lesson once a week. This situation makes it virtually impossible to give the visually-minded student sufficient help to waken the ears to active learning. There must be something to practice, so he is given notes to learn and finger drills. And thus we go on trying to help people to have access to this beautiful world of music without ever giving them a chance to work with its medium. When tone is the medium, what else is there to guide the learning process, except: How does it sound?

Having excellent critical ears and having learning ears is not necessarily the same thing. But learning ears are necessary if the individual is to have a satisfying musical experience with an instrument. Necessary, perhaps I should say, if there is to be ultimate security and joy with the instrument. The ears are not always able, at the beginning, to retain the sound image. The student with high scholastic attainments may not use his ears in acquiring knowledge, and may consequently have a difficult time with a musical skill. Yet, as a vital part of his education, no one would deprive him of the experience of making music for himself.

Two elements are the fundamental factors in learning a musical skill: the auditory image and the feeling of rhythm. They are completely fused when the instrument is a perfect medium for emotional expression. That fusion of the auditory image and the feeling of the rhythm should be the goal in all teaching. Every lesson should deal with the sound of the music and the feeling of its rhythm. Give the ears a chance to register tone by a long period of rote learning, and the body a chance to feel the exhilarating rhythm of music by a great deal of pantomime.

It is important that there is a clear understanding that two rhythms are always present in music: the rhythm of form and the rhythm of note values. The rhythm of form carries the legato feeling, the continuous telling of the story. The rhythm of articulation is the rhythm of separate movements. Playing most easily represents the creative musical ideas when the rhythm of form, the legato feeling, is the outlet for the surge of emotion. Let the body experience the lilt of the phrase before the attention is riveted on accuracy in hitting the right keys. The rhythmic experience that involves the torso as well as the hands lays a foundation for both beauty and ease.

The sensation of a body rhythm is illuminating; talking about it is pretty futile. There should be the relation between the center of the body and the hands that there is between the hub and the spokes of a wheel, or between the center and outside pins of a compass. They move in rhythmic harmony. Though the movements at the center of the body may be very tiny, let the feeling there of suspended energy, the continuity in activity, pick up the emotional response to the music. By taking pains to have the body experience the rhythmic continuity of form, the same kind of unbroken rhythm that a smooth skater enjoys, the pianist most easily gives forth a lilting phrase. Unless we deal with the streamline rhythm of form at the beginning, we allow the first impressions, which are the most lasting, to be those of the struggling movements of hitting right keys. When an unbroken rhythm is the counterpart of the continuous aural imagery, musical ideas most easily flow into tone. Pianists good and bad can almost be lined up in two classes. The good ones find the outlet for emotion through the rhythm of form carried in the body; and the bad ones find the emotional outlet in the rhythm of hitting the keys, carried in the hand.

No matter what the musical gifts may be, the results in presenting musical ideas depend on the body-coordination being right for producing the ultimate in subtlety in rhythmic nuance and gradation in the intensity of tone. These two tools of expression, rhythm and dynamics, cannot be achieved in their infinite variation except when the odds are for, instead of against, a smooth flowing rhythm. A curve produced by one long stroke is graded more minutely than a curve built by small digits. Gradation in intensity is most delicate when tones are produced by a continuous flow of energy and not when tones are produced by separate initiations of power. Listen to the gradation in tone when you are idly humming a tune. The intensity of the tone changes constantly. There is no need to regulate the breath. It varies automatically with the lilt of the tune. The pianist must train to have a continuous flow of tone-producing power that is completely fluid and sensitive, like the breath for song, so that all that is needed is a musical idea to have constant variation in the intensity of tone.

It is here that the special difficulty of the piano lies. It is a musical difficulty. We sit outside of our instrument, and we must produce tone through a vertical action, when the musical idea is the result of the succession of tones running laterally along the keyboard. We should be involved emotionally with the feeling of continuity, and instead, too often, we are involved with the feeling of the separate key-hitting strokes. And here is a real snag: The expertness of the hand as a tool, its enormous capacity for a sensitive movement, coupled with the fact that it contacts tone, makes the movements of the hand an easy outlet for the pianist's emotion; but the hand alone is incapable of playing the modern piano without strain, and there is no way of involving the whole body except through a coordination from the center to the outside. Beginning at the ends does not involve the middle but beginning at the middle does involve the ends. If the rhythm of form is sufficiently alluring to start activity in the torso, and these movements become the outlet for the emotional response to the music, we kill two birds with one stone. We have the chance for the greatest beauty because there is the possibility for an unbroken rhythm, and we have the greatest ease because the whole body, with the power of the large muscles, can be involved in producing successive tones.

Pick out the first-chair men in your orchestra. Doubtless they are first-chair men because their music is full of subtleties. Watch one of them when he has a solo to play. The minute that he, instead of the conductor, is responsible for the beauty of the music, something happens in his body. It suddenly picks up every rhythmic nuance, or, saying it the other way round — which I suspect is much nearer the truth — the body, by becoming completely light and buoyant and full of activity, creates the rhythmic nuance which you hear. It is never still, but constantly vibrates in response to the message the ear is registering. The manner of playing a theme and variations may serve as an illustration of the value of this central rhythm as the outlet for the emotional response to music. The theme is the musical idea in its simplest statement. The variations fit into the form of that statement. When they are beautifully played that form is never distorted. Just the reverse happens when they are badly played. That is, the change in the rhythmic pattern of tones is more important emotionally to the player than the continuous, long pattern of the form; and the variations are easily distorted into a series of small, almost unrelated pieces, instead of each variation being an integrated part of the composition as a whole. As listeners, we are bored in one instance and delighted in the other, for we become fatigued instead of thrilled when there is a welter of detail rather than a flowing rhythm, linking all the motives into one graceful line of progression.

When rhythm and dynamics are the vital tools of expression, as with the piano, the greatest subtlety in presenting ideas is achieved only when the body is coordinated as a whole, with the power and the rhythm starting at the center and flowing to the outside where tone is contacted.

Creative musical ideas cannot be transmitted to students, but the channel through which ideas may flow freely into tone can be taught. The formula is fairly simple to state, even though the sensitive balance of perfection evades complete analysis. The student must learn through the ear, and the body must be trained to have a continuous rhythm which is both the channel for the emotional outlet and the whip-handle for the power.

Flaws in Traditional Teaching of Piano *

❧❧

Educators, in general, have discarded many of the procedures that musicians still retain. Tradition has played an important role in the field of music, but does not justify clinging to unproductive tools in teaching.

As teachers of a skill, we have failed to evaluate the tremendous capacity of the body for achieving perfection in action and have allowed intellectual concepts to interfere with our taking advantage of the body's natural capacity for coordination, for results. The jazz player's accomplishments in facility and brilliance are formidable and, in many cases, the result not of study but of his good ears and innate rhythm. It is the magic worked by the right kind of rhythm that made his learning fast and efficient, a rhythm that has the basic quality of continuity in action, that stops for nothing, all details being absorbed in its stride, which is as continuous as the movement of the slow-motion picture. It flows along from the first tone to the last, and no movement for producing tone disturbs it. It is always in this sense of continuity in action, related to and highlighting the form of the composition, that I use the word rhythm.

Here is a list of flaws in traditional teaching which, in my opinion, are both wasteful and unproductive:

* It has been impossible to determine precisely when A. W. wrote this article, but internal evidence suggests a period when she was still working on her *Indispensables of Piano Playing*. [Eds.]

I. *The use of note values as a basis for rhythm.*

Musical perception, facility, and ease, the desirables in the making of beautiful music, are inevitably and indissolubly associated with the motor patterns that form the rhythm.

No more devastating habit can be formed than that of associating the rhythm of playing with the action for producing single tones. It should be associated with the action for progression, which can automatically absorb key depression. Only when there is a physical counterpart of the form or idea of the composition can the ear attend to the larger relationships of form. Continuity in action makes a relief map of the whole structure. The rhythm which is to be such a factor in the development of the student is almost entirely registered through muscle action.

The first habits may very easily condition the kind of rhythm to be used. With note values used as the basis for procedure, the action that produces each succeeding tone will be the only action there is to register the rhythm. The lapse of continuity in action negates an unbroken rhythm, which is the only sufficiently creative factor to tap the body's full capacity for coordination. Without that complete coordination perfection cannot be achieved.

Building up a measure by adding note values, one to the other, balks even the simple result of perfect note values. Note values can only be perfected in duration and be meaningful when they fill an already established larger unit of time. Establishing the larger unit of time, say the measure, means an awareness through continuity in action for that time unit. The subdivision of a large unit of time relates each tone forward, because subdivision presupposes that there is the concept, as well as a physical awareness, of the large time unit to be divided. Addition only relates the tones to what has gone before. No subtle beauty in performance can ever be achieved by such a relationship of tones. There must be a complete concept of the musical idea in order to relate each tone to what follows. This postulates a physical action which, dealing with large units of form as a whole, dominates the action for detail. Only a rhythm based on continuity of progression can foster the attention on the whole instead of the parts.

Attention to note values, before there is a physical habit of progression established, can dissipate the idea as a whole because movements are made to produce individual tones without their being related to the movement of continuous progression.

II. *Establishing habits of practice based from the start on a preoccupation with details.**

In the field of education the concept of the whole is all that is asked for at the beginning. Large movements are used before small movements are attempted. Detail must contribute to, not dissipate, the concept of the whole. This means, when learning a skill, that there must be action in muscles that deal with the large form, and that these motor habits must be formed first. Then the muscle actions that deal with the details can fit into and be absorbed by the action that deals with continuous progression.

For the painter, the size of the canvas determines the relationship of all the details. For the pianist, space perception is duration of time, and duration of time is shared by hearing and muscle action. It is the muscle action that produces continuity in progression and develops space perception to its greatest subtlety.

It is the kind of habits of action acquired in producing the kind of rhythm used that largely determines growth in the perception of music. If habits deal first with details, the conception of the music will probably deal with details, and the ears will listen for detail. Such procedure does not make for simplicity and clarity in the musical statement and it can wreck the coordination for

* See Details in Glossary.

the long line of progression. Attending to details first can so clutter up a musical statement that no audience can maintain attention to the performance. In acquiring habits put first things first.

To be aware of the composition as a whole, a physical action of continuity from the beginning to the end, with no stopping for details, is the thing to receive first attention, in order to foster the conception of the whole structure. No space perception can be refined without this procedure, and without that refinement no subtle beauty can be projected.

III. *Ear training stressed for its relation to musicianship without the full realization of its relation to motor controls.*

If habits of listening and habits of movement were not so interdependent, the lack of aural control of movement would not be so important. After years of effort visual learners, even after achieving a degree of success in playing while alone, are often almost helpless when they want to play for others. This helpless state, an uncontrollable nervoussnes, is very largely due to the fact that the whole playing process was put together by visual control. But, only the ear can most dependably form the aural image when sound is the medium; if the ear, lacking a clearly etched aural image, does not direct the movement which produces the tone, there will never be any real security in coordination or in memory.

Ear training must directly relate the perception of sounds with the performing activity which produces these sounds. When movement is motivated by the desire to produce what is heard, the aural image and the motor patterns will support each other. Little of value to the performer is accomplished in ear training classes when there is no associated muscular action. When movement is the result of a desire to make the imaged music come to life, known as playing by ear, then the control that allows the body to function with security is being used.

All of the expert public performers are aural learners, and from my experience I can say that an overwhelming majority have absolute pitch. Only the ear can skillfully direct the action that produces music.

Ear training should begin with the first lesson by allowing the pupil to learn the keyboard by the sound it produces, so that movement is for the sole purpose of producing the sounds that make music.

IV. *Traditional finger training — Independence of fingers — Striving for equal hitting power.*

On the basis of facility and ease, quite apart from what it does to beauty in performance, no procedure could be more wasteful of time spent at the piano than that of training fingers for production of tone. Perfection in playing demands the assistance that nature gives when the natural channels for learning, ear and rhythm, are used. Again, note the jazz player's facility, accuracy, and ease. Using only his ears and a smoothly functioning rhythm, he achieves his results without five-finger exercises and has fun in the process.

Coordination for a fully effective action takes place from the center of the radius of activity to the periphery; for playing, this means from the shoulder to the tips of the fingers (not from the fingers to the shoulder). If fingers are trained to reach for the keys, this reaching action tends to have the finger activity disengaged from a concerted action. Any habit which interferes with the completely coordinated action multiplies all the difficulties inordinately.

Reaching for lateral distance with the fingers is in itself sufficient cause for inaccuracy and difficulty with an intricate pattern. Reaching, gauging distance with the finger tips, changes the entire feeling of lateral distance at the keyboard. Picture the action of a compass: The center pin merely turns around while the outside arm travels the entire circumference of the circle. Distance controlled at the center of the radius of activity, the shoulder joint, has a very similar relation to the distance the hand travels in lateral progression, as the center pin to the outside arm of the compass. There is no distance at the shoulder joint, merely a turning at the joint. This gives the capacity for gauging distances accurately while maintaining a secure stance.

Control of distance at finger tips feels as different from control at the shoulder joint as the feeling of strain does from the feeling of ease. The former makes for difficulty and struggle while the latter assures facility and ease. The upper arm merely turns and gauges distance while all the other levers quite naturally and easily fit into the arm action controlled at the shoulder joint. Unfortunately, no one can have the joy and relief of this easy control at once. Once fingers have been trained to reach for position they hold onto that control tenaciously.

The distance the hand must travel at the keyboard is great, but, quite literally, that distance feels shortened, like an accordion when it is closed, when the control of distance is taken over by the shoulder joint. Difficulties in gauging distance that have been insurmountable simply vanish when the shoulder joint is actually in control of lateral progression. This matter of lateral distance is never solved with security when the fingers reach for position. The fingers must move as a part of central control if lateral distance is not to be a problem forever. Reaching with the fingers can prevent an easy coordination for distance from ever taking place. Training fingers to produce the power for tone puts a burden upon small muscles that all too frequently results in neuritis.

The fingers can never be made equal in hitting strength, nor can they furnish sufficient power for the range in dynamics of the modern piano. There is a fallacious argument that fingers control delicacy in shading. But, nothing is farther from the truth. To prove this, play a pianissimo scale with the fingers and then play a pianissimo glissando. The glissando operates with one control, the pull at the shoulder, and it is easy to keep it pianissimo. The scale with the fingers multiplies the difficulties tremendously without adding to the control of pianissimo. If the pull of the glissando is maintained in all playing, simply changing the direction of the pull so that it is toward the torso, and the finger action which is necessary to take key-drop is a coordinated part of that power produced by the pull, delicate shading is easy to achieve. This training of the fingers for producing tone is largely responsible for the terrific waste in playing talent. As a result of such training, piano playing always remains a struggle. To keep the machinery in anything like good playing condition, a daily workout is necessary. With a balanced, coordinated power for tone the playing mechanism does not fall apart the minute it is not used. It will stand a long vacation and remain unimpaired.

It is only a misconception that fingers cannot be as skilled in action if not trained for independence. They achieve just as precise an action when they operate as a part of the arm. It is merely a different action. It never makes sense to establish a habit that not only is not needed but that will interfere in achieving the required total coordination for playing. Training the completely coordinated arm will insure the cooperation of hand and fingers. Training the hand and fingers for independence does not insure complete cooperation of the arm.

V. *Playing scales to develop fluency, accuracy, and beauty.*

I know of no daily routine of scale playing that does not depend upon fingers for producing tone and that does not try to control dynamics with that power. The fact that such scale practice bores a child is reason enough for not using it, but the entire procedure is faulty for achieving facility and ease with the least expenditure of effort. A glimpse at the mechanism for easy fluency may suggest the reasons why the right controls for power and distance will produce brilliant scale playing, but scale practice will not contribute to the right controls. Both power and distance are, of necessity, controlled at the shoulder joint if there is to be access to a real fortissimo and the full width of the keyboard. Control for pianissimo or any in-between gradation is greatly facilitated by full-arm control. Control at shoulder joint means one control for both arms, a pull toward the body, a pull that throws all other movements into line in much the same manner in which the pull on the end of a lariat held in the hand determines all the movements made by the other end of the rope.

On the other hand, control by finger power means a complex set of controls. There are ten fingers to be controlled. When parallel motion is used the stronger fingers oppose the weaker ones. When the thumb passes under in one hand the fingers are passing over in the other. Parallel scales with finger power furnish every possible obstacle for easy coordination. With great effort one may learn to play the scale very well, using only finger power; but, such learning will not build a coordination that will be effective for all technical demands. Actually, it will only establish habits that make all other technical patterns harder to achieve.

Quite apart from the technical aspect, routine scale playing contributes materially in destroying the awareness that a scale is a musical pattern of great beauty. All tone-by-tone procedure negates the rhythm of the long line without which there is never any real simplicity nor great beauty in a musical statement.

VI. *Hanon and Czerny exercises.*

Czerny has been responsible for untold boredom, and that is exactly why his exercises should be discarded. Creativeness in ideas is fostered by response to beauty, not to boredom. It is time we learned to use beautiful music for achieving results if we are interested in producing beautiful playing.

Hanon is used for developing independent fingers with equal hitting power. Obviously this cannot be accomplished. Each finger may gain more power, but there will still be inequality in the fingers. Fingers need to be expert only in transmitting the power of the arm. That is a different and far simpler problem, which does not demand mechanical and uninteresting patterns.

The transmission of power to the key is the result of muscle energy made effective by the bony structure. If there were not the resistive value of the bone, no muscle action could be effective. The ligamentous attachment at the joints holds the bones together without strain. Even the little finger can bear tremendous power, but when it alone is used to produce tone it is ineffective. Certainly it cannot produce a fortissimo.

Why spend dull hours with Hanon when the arm can easily furnish all the power that is needed without specialized training? If we could only believe in nature's way instead of in traditional concepts, so much wasted time, boredom, and ultimate frustration could be avoided.

VII. *Breaking down difficult patterns into small details.*

So far as I can discover, all such practicing is based on the assumption that the difficulties in the pattern are caused by relationships in the use of the hand and fingers — with their control of lateral spacing and power for tone. The difficulty really lies in the fact that fingers are being used for controls for which they are inadequate. This kind of practice will not be needed anyway if the following things are borne in mind and acted upon:

(*a*) The control at shoulder joint gauges the activity of all the levers of the arm and hand.

(*b*) The rhythm of the musical idea is more important in acquiring the habits related to the learning of a piece than accuracy in detail.

(*c*) Direction in progression is a very important factor in making an intricate pattern easy. The direction of progression at the shoulder joint does not change for irregularities (in direction) in the line. It proceeds in the direction of the long line of the pattern.

(*d*) Arm power coordinates all the action of forearm,

hand, and fingers. Fingers take the key-drop and produce the tone. They must not get to the tone before the arm power. They do not take over the control of lateral progression, but merely synchronize with the shoulder-joint control.

Accuracy of the aural image is ultimately essential. Along with the accurate aural image, the above principles must be used if technical difficulties are to be resolved. Detailed work at patterns, such as the Cortot Edition of the Chopin Etudes suggests, will not bring the same results at all.

VIII. *Routine drill for beauty in performance.*

Routine drill dulls rather than stimulates the emotional reaction that is a part of all beautiful playing. The actual balance and play of movement change under the stimulation of emotional excitement. Beauty in performance involves the emotional reaction to the music being played. Habits formed through contact with beautiful music are not the same as habits established through routine drill. Habits that are established without emotional excitement will take their toll in the ultimate performance. It is strange that people so readily believe that joy in achieving results cannot turn the trick but that there must be boring drill. There must be repetition but not that of mechanical action. I am certain that a rhythm of form which becomes the channel for expressing the emotional reaction to music is the most creative factor that can be used for developing both facility and perception. This emotional rhythm is the antithesis of routine drill, and it works like a charm.

IX. *Slow practice for speed and accuracy.*

This, too, has to do with forming habits that are not those demanded by a performance. If the tempo of performance is practiced only after slow practice has made the accuracy of detail important, the habits are for slow detail — not for exciting performance. Also, slow practice does not perfect the blend in activity that is necessary for speed; it establishes habits of slow plodding. The right kind of slow practice (and even then, in moderate quantities only) can be useful for establishing new controls to replace faulty habits. A full-arm stroke (this can only be done in a slow tempo) can be used for each tone in studying a new composition. This makes it possible to form an auditory image while avoiding a physical action which is faulty for speed. Using the full-arm stroke means that the action for taking the key-drop is controlled at the shoulder where the circular joint makes it possible to maintain continuity in action. Note that this action should always be staccato to assure buoyancy.

A tempo slow enough for close observation and a fully controlled action can be useful for substituting a new habit for an old one. But the widespread and well-established belief that slow practice is the right and definitely superior way of practicing, which will cure all ills, is far removed from the truth. Slow practice, especially when it is legato, may permit the establishing and constant strengthening of habits which inhibit beauty and the easy flow of music. The goals we are working for have to do with just that, beauty and a fluid grace. Favor these goals at every contact with your instrument.

Any time that habits are formed which do not meet the requirements for performance, we have lessened the chances of ever achieving that performance. The physical counterpart of a beautiful performance should be used as nearly as possible at the first reading. The music can still shine through, in spite of omissions and some wrong tones, if a tempo is used that fits its beauty, and an emotional rhythm brings all the important harmonies into relief.

X. *Initial slow practice for accuracy before using a musical tempo.*

The demand for accuracy in key hitting, at the expense

of a coordinated action for an emotional performance, fails to put first things first. Is accuracy more important than a beautiful statement? If that were true the concert halls would be filled for dozens and dozens of performances, for there are plenty of players who can hit all the keys accurately. But without beauty in their playing there is no clamoring audience for their second season. Accuracy, of course, cannot be ignored, but it can be better achieved after the musical conception has jelled. If a beautiful performance is the ultimate goal, then the elements that produce that beauty must have first place in attention and, thus, condition first habits. Let beauty work its charm first. Only rhythmic continuity that makes for a connected sequence of the important structural skeleton can project, as well as further, a beautiful conception. It is only the rhythm of form that helps the first reading to find the relationships in the music that make for the simplicity of the inspired performance. Practice which uses rhythmic progression clarifies and beautifies the musical statement. The demand for accuracy in hitting the keys forces attention on single tones and does not allow the attention to skim through for the important ideas and, thus, develop the physical habits that are right for projecting the musical idea as a whole. That demands the tempo in which the music was conceived. Later, a slow tempo for observation of what causes the technical difficulties will be less likely to establish a faulty coordination when the tempo of a real performance is used.

XI. *Relaxation for effortless and beautiful playing.*

Relaxation is *not* the physical basis for a superlative performance. The readiness for action in playing demands a balanced coordination as the stance for movement. It is the coordination of the cat waiting to pounce upon his prey rather than the relaxation of the cat asleep in the sun. This readiness, suspension, balance in activity, and alertness is a necessary and vital part of rhythmic continuity, without which neither speed, ease, nor beauty are fostered. If what is meant by relaxation is absence of all strain, then it is right, but it suggests "letting go."* Releasing or letting go in the motive power is one of the most deadly habits a pianist can acquire. Releasing completely balks the developing of a continuous rhythm. I can almost say that beauty in performance is related to the absence of release. Releasing means emphasizing individual tones and lack of continuity.

XII. *Relationship of tone quality to touch in piano playing.*

The scientist is on one side of this argument concerning tone quality, and the emotional musician on the other. The scientist knows that to influence the tone quality the energy producing the tone must contact the string which produces the vibrations that create the tone. The musician has an emotional reaction to the music which becomes associated with the feel of the key as well as the sound of the tone. The facts are: A felt hammer hits the string and sets the string vibrating; this vibration produces the tone; the player is not in contact with the vibrating string; all he can do is to make the felt hammer strike the string with greater or lesser force. There will be a certain quality for each intensity of tone, but the player cannot separate the two. The quality was determined by the manufacturer of the instrument. The pianist can control two attributes of the piano tone: duration and intensity. But, quality can only be influenced by the performer who contacts the tone-producing mechanism, as the violinist or singer does.

The mechanism of the piano produces the noises of percussion involved with the key action, but those noises are not part of the tone produced by the vibrating string. However, they are the reason for all the adjectives used in connection with criticism, such as hard, harsh, brittle, etc. In a small room these noises are very evident and

* See Glossary.

often disturbing. In the concert hall we hear tone without these noises, unless we are too close to the instrument. There is a relationship between the volume of tone and these percussive noises. Loudness is produced by the speed with which the energy is delivered. This speed makes the impact with the key bed very strong, and it is this impact, primarily, that causes the noise that is disliked. The impact is lessened when the energy for tone is aimed for a level just above key bed. This may be checked by watching the hammers. If the power for a fortissimo chord, for instance, is snapped against the key so that the peak of the snap happens just before the key bed is reached, 'and there is no holding of the power against the key bed, but immediate progression, the hammers will flutter a bit after they hit the string. If the power is aimed at key bed, it will mean a longer contact with the key bed, and the hammers will not flutter after they hit the string. This fast and accurate delivery of power is of great value for both speed and conservation of energy, but it does not change the quality of tone.

XIII. *Legato and staccato as basis for phrasing. Is there a legato touch and staccato touch?*

Legato and staccato need redefining as they are related to piano playing. For singer and string player, connecting tones produce an entirely different effect from the connection of piano tones. The actual holding of the tone with the breath or the bow is an expression of the emotional reaction involved with the music, because the dynamics are controlled throughout the holding process. This is not so with the piano. Holding the key down can produce no increase of volume and cannot prevent the piano tone from diminishing in intensity.

Any projection of emotion, through the use of dynamics, must deal with the intensity of tones at the moment of production. It is this relation of the intensity of tones at the moment of their inception that almost entirely conveys the feeling of legato. Thus, tonal relationships are more meaningful at the piano not through key connection but through gradation in the energy used at the moment of tone production. But, to a large extent, both critics and lay listeners believe that it is key connection which produces their feeling of legato playing, when in reality they are reacting almost entirely to the manner in which the dynamics are used.

In slow playing there are times when the pedal is not desirable. Then, the key must be held down to prolong the duration of the sound. But, in fast or moderate speeds it is dynamics that produce the sense of legato. Harold Samuels' playing of Bach is proof of this; tones were rarely connected, but the grace of his rhythm produced a subtlety in the handling of dynamics that made the music flow in a delightful manner.

Staccato, which is defined as detached and is so with the breath or bow, is frequently used for emphasis alone in editing for the piano. For example, note how often staccato and damper pedal are indicated at the same time. The pedal completely negates the detachment. One learns by experience to judge whether detachment or emphasis (or both) is desired.

As to tone production, there is not the slightest difference between staccato and legato at the piano except in duration. The piano tone has only two attributes controlled by the performer: duration and intensity. Duration is controlled by keeping the key depressed or by the use of the damper pedal. The string is kept free to vibrate in both instances. If the key is not held down it comes up. Shortness, for staccato, is regulated by the energy used for tone rather than with an action of coming off the key. Associate "staccato" with the positive action of tone production, rather than with the negative action of getting away from the key after the tone has been produced. It is power used for a short duration of time that produces staccato. It is not a certain kind of up-action with finger, hand, or arm. All too often, pupils are trained in these up-actions not only for staccato, but for separating phrases as well. Some believe there is no good phrasing without them. Nothing could be farther from the truth. Phrases are beautiful in proportion to the subtlety with which rhythmic nuance and dynamics are used.

XIV. *Editing and the meaning of the music.*

Editing has been a matter of great controversy. If editing is so important, why is it that so many people can play from the same page with totally different results? They may all attend to all of the prescribed details that editing indicates and still produce completely different results.

The truth is that editing, by itself, is helpless to produce anything that is remotely related to a beautiful performance. Only a long, rhythmic line can sufficiently assist the performer to produce the subtlety in rhythmic nuance and dynamics demanded for beauty. Once a rhythm of form is in possession of the playing, the music will make sense without editing. It is only when there is this rhythm in the body that good editing does make sense. A good editor, in my opinion, does very little editing. Editing should be called to the attention of the student only after a sensitive, continuous rhythm has been established. Then it is an asset, but when used to create a performance it forms another distraction from the most vital necessity — the rhythm of form.

XV. *Musical style and specialized technical demands.*

What determines the style of a composer? What are his means of expression? They are only tonal combinations, form, and rhythm. It is his individual manner of combining these elements that determines his style. It is true that there is a traditional manner of playing embellishments in music written for the harpsichord, but this manner does not demand a specialized finger technique. It simply demands clarity and rhythmic proportion, as does all music. In all too many instances we have substituted intellectual concepts for the use of an "emotional rhythm." One factor, more than any other, is responsible for real rapport with Haydn and Mozart. It is not the kind of staccato or legato, nor a special finger action, but it is a sensitive, flowing, unbroken rhythm of form. I do not mean to imply that the performance of modern composers does not suffer equally from a lack of this rhythm, but audiences are apt to think that it is the composition rather than the performance that they dislike, because they are less familiar with the modern idiom. The same music could create a totally different effect if skillfully projected through an unerring rhythm.

The romantic composers need a flexible, rhythmic nuance — not unduly exaggerated. This is not gained by an intellectual grasp of their style but, rather, by the physical equipment which, when used rhythmically, heightens all musical perception. The results that allow music to speak with all its innate charm, no matter what the style or period, are always related to the kind of rhythm that saturates the being of the performer and not to any specialized kind of physical approach. Every student is pretty helpless in finding the inner meaning of any composer without this rhythm. With it, his understanding of all composers and all art forms is greatly enhanced.

XVI. *Coaching and performance.*

We need to learn that facts, as related to skills, become pertinent and usable only when the body has learned the movements that produce the right results. It is the doing that teaches students the facts. The intellectual concept is not meaningful without the experience of achievement. Repeatedly I have had students say to me, "The page does not look the same; I never heard it that way before," after they had sensed the long, rhythmic line.

Coaching is supposed to deal with interpretation. This

implies that one handles the manner of using shading, retards, accelerandos, specific ways of turning a phrase, etc. Coaching almost exclusively involves attention to discriminating listening, so that the student can skillfully imitate the master. In order to do this the student must have the same kind of physical equipment as the master has, as well as the discriminatory ear. This is the reason why he frequently does not profit from expert coaching. The coach may demonstrate the beauty of a phrase, but he does not deal with the physical basis of producing this beauty — at least not enough to rectify the faulty physical habits of the student and to supply him with the same controls for power, distance, and rhythm that the master uses. I have no doubt that the master is almost always unaware of what physical coordination he uses when he plays. His ears have been in command of his performance for a long time. That is all that is needed, when physical habits are right, for beauty in performance. The aural image furnishes an idea, and the body is directed by that idea. Why bother with the manner of tying your shoe lace when you can so easily tie it? But the unfortunate student, with physical habits that bungle his performance, cannot use the aural image so expertly. His ear, no matter how discriminating, is helpless to achieve results — the kind of results that are only possible when the mechanism no longer bungles. An authoritative and beautiful performance demands both discriminating ears and a highly developed rhythm that takes away all strain. Skillful use of the aural image and the ability to register the elements of beauty that are imaged are indissolubly wedded to this rhythmic continuity. Coaching must deal with both ears and rhythm to be truly effective. When it does, it will have turned into expert teaching.

Glossary

Alternating Action: There is a long description in this book. Keep in mind that the upper arm should always participat and coordinate all activity through its pull or holding action But, the term "alternating action" refers specifically to the interaction between the forearm and hand, and not to what happens in the upper arm.

Alternating action permits tone to be produced both when the forearm extends, as well as when it flexes. There is no wasted motion. For example, if the hand is kept in the same relation to the forearm, the latter, after producing tone, must come up before it can again descend and strike the key — there is a wasted action in this, one which merely moves away from the key. Using alternating action, the forearm can participate in striking the key *while it (the forearm) is coming up.*

Note that after the forearm has been extended (wrist low), and, thus, has taken a large share of the articulation, it rises — flexes (wrist high), but the hand, by flexing at this point, tilts towards the key and strikes it, assisted physically by the very rise or flexion of the forearm (and again the upper arm supervises the entire procedure). One flexion or one extension, combined with the pull of the upper arm and the rotary action of the forearm, need not produce just one tone; whole groups of consecutive tones can easily be produced by one such action.

Articulation: Used in relation to the piano, the word refers to the vertical physical action or actions which move the key down to produce tone.

Bony, Bony Alignment, Bony Arch, Bone on Tone, On Bone, One Bone: an alignment of bones of the upper arm,

* See p. 40.

188

forearm, hand, and fingers at the point of tone production. The following is a definition once given by the author: "such a coordination of the various shafts of power so that at the moment that tone is produced there is a feeling of one bone from shoulder to finger tip."

Details: Although the word was sometimes used in connection with a short section of a composition, most of the time it referred to individual notes and the actions of articulation which were used to play these individual notes. An undue preoccupation with details meant that the ear was listening to each note in turn, and the actions of articulation were outside the stream of power which was responsible for producing a phrasewise progression.

Down in Front: This expression is really allied with another one, *sticking*. It implies that the fingers or hand are *ahead* of the upper arm in arriving at tone (producing tone); in addition, there is a completely wasteful pressure against the key bed after tone has been produced, when all that is called for, at that point, is keeping the key down so that tone may continue sounding.

Faulty Pitch: an inadequate perception of pitch — a poor relative pitch — which prevents the pianist from learning music easily.

First Lever: another name for the upper arm — the part of the arm extending from the shoulder joint to the elbow.

Focusing: the precise delivery of power at that point in the descent of the key where the hammer is tripped and strikes the strings, producing sound.

Full-arm Stroke: The full-arm stroke is one of the prime practicing tools by means of which the pianist can establish a coordination in which the upper arm is the dominant, controlling lever for playing the piano. The upper arm, forearm, and hand are kept in unchanging position in relation to each other while the upper arm moves to cover horizontal distance and swings in an arc down and towards the torso to strike the key. The forearm, hand, and fingers, by staying alert as a "bony extension of the upper arm," enable the power of the upper arm to be transmitted into tone. The full-arm stroke can only be used on successive tones in a slow-to-moderate tempo. By its very nature it would be unwieldy in even a moderately rapid tempo. The following pattern is very helpful for learning to use the full-arm stroke. For a balanced action, play with both hands an octave apart.

Ex.17

Thereafter this full-arm stroke is used for two purposes:
(1) to learn new music.
(2) to strengthen the coordination in which it is the upper arm, and not the fingers, which initiates finding the keys. If the upper arm initiates this action, it is that much more prone to dominate the entire coordination necessary for striking the keys as well. This coordination is essential for learning to use a basic rhythm.

Fussy Playing: a playing which is directed by ears which are too concerned with each individual sound, and a playing coordination more involved with actions of articulation than with the horizontal, phrasewise progression. Even the performer who habitually plays with a basic rhythm may, on occasion, be too preoccupied with individual notes. In either case the playing has too many changes in dynamics and lacks subtlety in timing.

Imagery: This is dealt with at length both in *Indispensables of Piano Playing,* and in this set of essays. Briefly, a desired, subtle coordination can be more easily and effectively brought about by means of a vivid word-picture, imaged action, than through a prosaic description. For instance, suggesting that the student imagine and pantomime holding a baby bird in his hand will make that hand gently alert much more easily than saying, "Make your hand alert."

Impulse, Playing Off of an Impulse: An impulse is a physical action which starts a continuous physical activity. It is the kind of push-off used by a boy who is running a race, or the swimmer who pushes off from the edge of a pool as he dives in to come up swimming. Playing off of an impulse refers to the activity which follows the push-off. Within a single composition, particularly a long one, there can be several impulses, one playing off of another, but there should never be so complete a stop that a totally fresh impulse is necessary.

Key Bed: the point in the descent of the key, beyond which it cannot go.

Key-drop: the motion of the key as it is struck to produce sound.

Key Level: that point in the descent of the key at which the hammer is tripped so that it strikes the strings and produces sound.

Kick-off or **Up-action:** a strong push-off from the keys, after striking them. This action is particularly likely to occur when the pianist plays fortissimo or staccato, or when a tone or chord is followed by a rest. A basic rhythm, marked by a strong sense of destination, will operate more effectively if all physical action is aimed *towards* tone and never *away* from it.

Legato, Legato Feeling: When this is used in reference to the upper arm, a feeling of smoothness in the motion of the upper arm is meant, rather than the usual concept of holding one key down until the next one is struck.

Letting Go: the opposite of *suspension* (see definition). It implies that, after tone has been produced, one relaxes or breaks the continuous activity of the upper arm on its way to a musical destination.

Lilt: Lilting on a note means that this is the note towards which one plays, or the note off of which one continues playing.

Outlining, Pulsing, Scanning: Outlining a composition means playing it sketchily — playing only the highlights, not including all the notes. The word *"outlining"* was the name first used for this procedure; although the other terms replaced it at times, it seems to have been more enduring.

At all times the tempo should be the one which permits the pianist to sense the mood and character of the music — in short, the tempo indicated by the composer. Taking a slower tempo, particularly in the case of lively compositions, would make it easier to find all the notes, but would also rob the music of its vitality. The author felt that the first acquaintance with a composition should be at a tempo which permits the intrinsic quality of the music to come through. Later, if there is need, one can play the music slowly. This need is dictated by the auditory equipment of the pianist. If his ears are very good and readily translate the printed symbols into an aural image, slow practice can be largely eliminated. If his ears do not translate the page into sound easily, slow practice has to be used, but the author felt that slow practice, by its very nature, can be harmful and should always be staccato, and thus "do the least damage." She felt that slow practice is conducive to a stodgy, notewise playing; if it were legato it would be that much more likely to result in a lethargic heavy-handedness.

If the pianist were to play all the notes of a completely new composition which required a lively or even rapid tempo, the task might frequently be beyond his means or, at the very least, the torrent of unfamiliar notes would produce strain and harassment. This is one reason for omitting notes. There are two others: By omitting some details (notes) the pianist is enabled to train his ears to "listen ahead." Just as we have to look where we are going, so should the pianist hear where he is going. Abby Whiteside was convinced that one of the important reasons for much dull playing, at the professional level, is the faulty habit that talented musicians are so likely to fall into of listening to each note individually, as it is produced, without any sense of aiming beyond the tone which is being produced. By omitting notes in the music which is being studied, the pianist is establishing in his ears a close association between notes in the music which are not next to each other. In the same way, outlining helps the pianist to develop an awareness of the large actions of the upper arms in tracing the large progressions both within a phrase or from phrase to phrase, rather than to be conscious solely of the actions of articulation.

Any pianist, beginner or advanced, can outline. He does have to become comfortable with this process, and it is essential, if he is to be successful, that he outline with the total involvement he would want to have in the final, polished performance. The omission of emotional involvement would make this a curious exercise which would not influence for the better his final performance.

The time unit in which just one chord or tone is played should be neither too short nor too long. If the unit is too short there will still be the pressure of having too many notes to play. On the other hand, if the measure is very long it is very difficult, at least at first, to fill it with a steady and smooth progression and actually to sense it as one, unbroken unit. Please note that one should not measure the length of any time unit by counting or by playing in one's head the notes which are being omitted. Both practices would largely negate the purpose of outlining.

Usually, in a moderate tempo, a bar of music provides a convenient unit. For instance, in the first movement of the Beethoven Sonata in D major, Op. 10, No. 3, one could start by playing the first quarter note of each measure and then add either the fourth or third quarter notes. But the second movement is much too slow to play only one eighth note (the first one) in each measure; it would be easier to play the first and the fourth beats. At the other extreme, the Brahms Capriccio in D minor, Op. 116, No. 1 is so fast, and the bars so brief, that playing the first chord in each measure might be quite difficult on a first reading. One ought to play one chord for every two-measure unit, or, even better, one chord for every four-measure unit. In the early stages of learning to outline, it would be best to choose music in which one bar is a convenient unit.

Patterns: The term is used in two ways. It refers to:

(1) The tonal pattern of a composition, for instance, the thirds and sixths of the Chopin Etude, Op. 10, No. 7, or the broken arpeggio patterns of Etude, Op. 25, No. 11.

(2) A form of practicing which uses either the C major scale or a chromatic scale to solve a number of musical problems: playing in time, outlining spontaneously (variation in the choice of notes to be included) to develop the kind of grace in performance which occurs only when there is a slow spacing underneath rapid and brilliant playing.

Use of patterns for time values

A.W. always used patterns starting on C. The size of the

interval used in the pattern depends on the time values involved. For example, if the fastest note is a sixteenth, and one wishes to establish the relationship of sixteenths, eighths, quarters — up to a half-note in length — one takes a ninth (the primary pattern). The sixteenth-notes are played as consecutive white keys. White keys, a third apart, would represent eighths. Quarter-notes would be a fifth apart, and the ninth white key stands for the beginning of the second half-note.

Ex.18

Primary pattern   Played

These two notes are played back and forth, staccato, with both hands an octave apart, until a given time unit is firmly established. The staccato permits a more vivid awareness of the duration because the two arms then can move in an exaggerated, smooth arc between the two tones. The duration can also be underlined by a swaying of the torso. Playing with both hands at the same time helps to balance the torso.

When the time unit is clearly established, the following patterns could be substituted to establish the time relationship of the various time values:

18 A

It is useful to return to the primary pattern frequently. The patterns should be played at various speeds. This practice is useful in solving any difficulties with time. The use of patterns is preferable to counting to establish awareness of metrical relations because a large time unit is established, both physically and aurally, before variations in details are tried. Thus, details or smaller time units are always felt as part of a larger entity. Counting starts and ends in preoccupation with detail. A flowing musical performance will usually be inhibited or completely prevented when the starting basis is involvement with detail.

Use of patterns for outlining

In his first attempts at outlining, the pianist will often find the process difficult because: (1) He can't easily decide which notes to omit. (2) The beauty of the music often makes it hard for him to omit anything. (3) A spontaneous selection of the notes to play is much more effective than a mechanical, pre-planned choice, but it can be very difficult at first because the notes are continuously changing as the composition progresses. The pattern is useful for acquiring this spontaneity because the notes which are played are chosen from the same unchanging set of scale tones. Because the scale pattern does not have an intrinsic tonal beauty, the pianist can much more easily become involved with the physical spacing between the beginning and the end of the pattern; it is the very involvement with the sensuous beauty of a composition which, paradoxically, can be responsible for producing a notewise listening and overinvolvement with each individual articulation.

The pattern is used as follows: Assume that the composition one is studying is in ¾ time, and the fastest notes are sixteenths. There can be twelve sixteenths in a bar, therefore the pianist takes the interval of a thirteenth, the last note of the interval representing the first note of the second measure. Each white key stands for a sixteenth-note (the consecutive white keys always represent whatever are the fastest notes of a given composition). Therefore, if one wants eighth-notes every other key is played; for quarter-notes, one plays the keys a fifth apart. The pattern and all the variations should be played in several speeds: first a moderate one, then a fast one, and then a slow speed — the last one is usually the hardest. Finally, the pattern should be played approximately in the speed of the composition which the pianist is studying.

First, playing with both hands an octave apart, the pianist swings his arms in a graceful arc from C to A.

Ex.19

Primary pattern

Please note that, no matter what the pianist tucks in on the way from C to A, he should take as long to come back to C as he did on the way to A. Thus, on the way back the pianist refreshes and further strengthens the awareness of the time unit for the measure, uncluttered by any tones between the outside ones. The choice of keys to be tucked in is enormous. A few examples:

Trying to find all sorts of variations within a given time unit makes the pianist much more comfortable with outlining a composition and the spontaneous choice of notes to be played, which outlining calls for.

Chromatic Scale Patterns (in Octaves)

Sometimes a chromatic scale is used to provide a smooth progression through some stubborn passage. The in-and-out motions of the upper arms, which are so readily stimulated by the arrangement on the keyboard of the black and white keys, make this pattern valuable. First one plays the scale in the speed of the fastest notes of the given passage, then one changes the metric pattern so that it is the same as the passage in question.

Pencil-lever or **Pencil:** one more name — used as imagery — for the upper arm.

Perfect Pitch, Learning Ears, Aural Person: The first term is obviously another name for absolute pitch, but, in general, these terms describe a person who learns aurally more readily than visually. Even musicians gifted with absolute pitch are not always prone to learn aurally. There were examples in the author's teaching experience of musicians with this ability who had been so conditioned to use their eyes, instead of their ears, that their ears did not dominate the learning process, and, frequently, they even had difficulty with memorizing.

Improvisation, learning by rote, and transposition were used to restore the ears to the dominant role which they should have in the learning of music.

Abby Whiteside was firmly convinced that aural learning should be nurtured by every possible means — learning by rote, transposition, etc. at the beginning of music study. She even felt that, for this purpose, the teacher should postpone as long as possible learning to read music.

Power, Power Stream: Using one's power implies a co-ordination in which the upper arm initiates the action of finding a key and dominates the action of striking it. Developing such a coordination is the first goal with every new student because one cannot begin to play with a basic rhythm until power is used with some consistency.

Pull, Hold, Holding: These terms are particularly difficult to define or make tangible. Traditional practicing habits tend to make it almost impossible for a pianist to conceive of the coordination described here as being possible.

As the pianist lowers his arms to have the fingers contact the keys, the upper arm actually moves toward the torso and, therefore, away from the piano. Abby Whiteside called this action *pulling*. The pianist who is learning to use this pulling or holding action often tends to pull much too hard. The pull must actually be very gentle and must be operative as long as one plays. What is essential is that this pull must be emotionally important to the pianist; only thus can it be the tool for making a beautiful musical statement. The fact that the shoulder joint is a ball joint and not a hinge joint makes it possible for the pull to be continuous. This physical continuity can coordinate and dominate all actions of articulation, and forms the basis for musical continuity.

Rhythm, Basic Rhythm, Rhythm of Form, Rhythm of Meter:

Rhythm or — interchangeably — **Basic Rhythm**: These were the terms used by the author to describe the continuous activity in the arms and torso which control the total physical apparatus as the performer plays a composition. She once gave this definition: "Rhythm is an emotionally involved power (see definition) which, in response to an auditory image, moves in a balanced, centered, lilting way towards a distant musical goal."

The words "emotionally involved" are of the utmost importance in Abby Whiteside's teaching. Practice produces habits. The pianist's goal is a beautiful performance, therefore one which is emotionally involved. Mechanical practice develops the habit of mechanical playing, which cannot readily be shaken off and therefore is always bad. The author felt that the pianist always had to be emotionally involved for practice to produce best results.

Rhythm of Form: the phrase-by-phrase progression in the music itself which is the guide for the basic rhythm in the performer's body.

Rhythm of Meter: refers to the organization of beats in a measure and the division within beats, note values, etc. All too frequently this is referred to as rhythm. Actually, it is but a detail of rhythm.

Slow Rhythm: a facet of playing with a rhythm. It is such a balanced use of the playing mechanism that there is no feeling of a sudden quickening or intensifying when the music becomes either faster or louder or, on the other hand, a slowing down or relaxing when the music becomes softer or slower. A slow rhythm becomes more and more perceptible as one becomes aware of spacing (see definition).

Spacing: deals with what the pianist does in between striking keys or articulating. It is an alive, continuous activity in the upper arm which can and should operate throughout the composition in the time-spaces between articulations of tones. In short, the actual muscular activity of striking the key should be the by-product of the activity which goes on in between the actions of articulation.

Stance: the position taken by the hand, arm, and torso as progression up or down the keyboard takes place.

Sticking: used to describe the energy-wasting and faulty procedure of continuing to press against the key bed after tone has been produced.

Suspension: After tone has been produced, especially a long tone, or when a tone is followed by a rest, there is a tendency to relax or *let go* (see definition). Suspension is the opposite of that. When power for tone is delivered, there is an instantaneous return to the same readiness for action which was there before the delivery.

Transfer: the name for a learning process which can be used either in teaching or in one's own practice. Whenever there is technical difficulty in playing or a lack of a graceful phrase-progression, one will find an upper arm which is not sufficiently active and peripheral levers — forearm, hand, and fingers — which are too active. This is the result of undue involvement with articulation. It is then necessary to increase the activity of the upper arm, so that it will govern and coordinate the actions of articulation. To accomplish this subtle change *transferring* is invaluable.

The teacher who has a basic rhythm and is very aware of how this rhythm feels can transfer, by various means, this awareness to the student. For instance, the teacher holds the student's hand, forearm, or upper arm. When the student reaches for the keys, the teacher can readily sense whether the upper arm is playing the dominant role, or whether the fore-arm, hand, or fingers are *ahead*. By checking the faulty motion through a gentle but firm opposition, he can make the student vividly conscious of where the action is strongest. Or, the student places his hand back of the teacher's upper arm, near the elbow, as the teacher plays, he can then feel how the upper arm is working. This can be remarkably effective, but success depends very much on the finesse in handling.

In his own practice the pianist works to attain an ever keener and more subtle awareness of the physical sensation of an unstrained, buoyant progression. For this purpose he may use an outline, a glissando, or playing a composition or passage where he knows that everything is going swimmingly, and a rhythm is in control. Having achieved this awareness, he carries it over to the composition where he is having difficulty. (See **Patterns.**)

Traveling: the name given to playing in which the ear does not listen far enough ahead, too many notes are made important, and there is overactivity of the "peripheral shafts of power" (forearm, hand, and fingers).

Twist, Untwist: the opposite directions of the rotary motion of the forearm. The more the forearm pronates, the more it twists; the more it supinates, the more it untwists.

Upper Arm: the part of the arm which extends from the shoulder joint to the elbow.

Vitalize: refers to the action of the fingers. They become alert so that the power of the upper arm can be delivered through them to the key, producing tone. But, they neither initiate the action of finding keys nor do most of the work of striking them.